THE FINE ART
OF THE
FURNITURE MAKER

THE FINE ART
OF THE
FURNITURE MAKER

CONVERSATIONS WITH WENDELL CASTLE, ARTIST,
AND PENELOPE HUNTER-STIEBEL, CURATOR,
ABOUT SELECTED WORKS FROM
THE METROPOLITAN MUSEUM OF ART

EDITED BY PATRICIA BAYER

PUBLISHED IN CONJUNCTION WITH AN EXHIBITION AT
MEMORIAL ART GALLERY
OF THE UNIVERSITY OF ROCHESTER
NOVEMBER 8-DECEMBER 27, 1981

All photographs except pages 8, 9, 35, 52, 53, and 66 copyright © 1981 by
The Metropolitan Museum of Art.

All color photographs except pages 19, 67, and 100 by Sheldan Collins,
Photography Studio, The Metropolitan Museum of Art. Page 100 by Walter Yee,
The Metropolitan Museum of Art.

Additional photo credits:
Page 8, top and bottom, courtesy Wendell Castle Inc., Scottsville, New York
Page 8, center, courtesy Alexander Milliken Gallery, New York
Page 9, photo by Gerald G. Stiebel
Page 35, courtesy Bayerische Staatsgemäldesammlungen, Munich
Page 52, courtesy Sotheby's New York
Page 53, courtesy Yale University Art Gallery, New Haven
Page 66, courtesy Mark Twain Memorial, Hartford

All other black and white photos courtesy Photography Studio, The Metropolitan
Museum of Art.

Library of Congress Catalog Card Number: 81-83164
ISBN 0-918098-10-6

Design and art direction by Mary Mullin

Printed by S.D. Scott Printing Company, Inc., New York

Typesetting by PM Coldtype Company, Inc., New York

Cover photograph by Sheldan Collins, The Metropolitan Museum of Art;
detail, Library Table by Herter Brothers; see page 55.

Published by Memorial Art Gallery of the University of Rochester, Rochester, New York.
Printed in conjunction with *The Fine Art of the Furniture Maker,* an exhibition
presented at the Memorial Art Gallery of the University of Rochester, November 8-
December 27, 1981. Sponsored in part by a grant from the New York State Council on
the Arts.

TABLE OF CONTENTS

FOREWORD BY BRET WALLER, DIRECTOR,
   MEMORIAL ART GALLERY OF THE UNIVERSITY OF ROCHESTER   6

INTRODUCTION TO ARTIST AND CURATOR   8

DISCUSSIONS OF OBJECTS   10

GLOSSARY   110

Note: All dimensions are given in inches.

FOREWORD

Before there were art historians there were artists, and it was universally understood that artists could have something perceptive to say about art. But in our own time, with the emergence of art history as an independent academic discipline, artists have been gradually disenfranchised; the art of the past has become the province of art historians, while artists, when consulted at all, are asked only to comment on their own work, or at most on the work of their contemporaries. The dialogue about art has tended toward art historical monologue; modern artists have fallen mute in the presence of the Old Masters and the public has been deprived of an alternate view of the art of the past.

Recently, however, there have been encouraging signs of change. Artists once again are looking at and talking about works that lie outside the accepted modernist canon. Their judgments are not anti-historical, but ahistorical, based on immediate personal response to the thing itself; artists tend to view all art as if it were contemporary. The artist's direct, unmediated approach cannot substitute for the historian's patient effort to understand the work of art in the context of its age and culture, but it may provide a useful corrective to the historian's occasional tendency to value context above content. And the two approaches taken together can help us see and understand the work of art in its full historical and aesthetic dimensions. An artist's view of the art of the past likewise sheds light on the artist's own work and the sources of his or her inspiration.

The present exhibition is a case in point. It had its origin in an observation by Wendell Castle to the effect that as he has matured as an artist his interest in the historical tradition of fine cabinetmaking has broadened to include works in styles he once found completely un-congenial. From this initial impetus, and thanks to the generous cooperation of the Metropolitan Museum, the exhibition has grown. The objects discussed in the catalogue have been drawn entirely from the Metropolitan's own extensive reserve collections to which the artist was given free access and permitted to select works he found aesthetically satisfying, instructive, or otherwise interesting. A few desirable works, particularly eighteenth century French pieces, because of their fragility, could not travel. And because so much of the Metropolitan's best American furniture is now on exhibition in the newly opened American Wing, early American furniture is not represented. Otherwise the selection represents the artist's free choice circumscribed only by the limits of the Metropolitan's holdings.

Although the selections were made entirely by Wendell Castle, the project could not have been realized without the full and enthusiastic participation of Penelope Hunter-Stiebel, Associate Curator of

Twentieth Century Art, who made all the necessary arrangements for access and escorted the artist through the Metropolitan's labyrinthian storerooms. The text of this catalogue, cast in the form of a dialogue between art historian/curator Hunter-Stiebel and artist/craftsman Castle, makes clear the central importance of Mrs. Hunter-Stiebel's participation. The dialogue was, in fact, recorded during the two days in which final object selections were made. It has been transcribed and edited by Patricia Bayer, who also has overseen production of the catalogue by working closely with all the participants and with graphic designer Mary Mullin.

For the extraordinary cooperation extended by the Metropolitan Museum we are indebted, first of all, to Philippe de Montebello, Director of the Metropolitan, and Deputy Director James Pilgrim, both of whom responded positively to our initial, tentative inquiries. Needless to say, without their full support the exhibition could not have come about.

I also wish to acknowledge the generous assistance rendered by staff members of the several curatorial departments from which the objects in the exhibition have been drawn: Department of Twentieth Century Art, William S. Lieberman, Chairman; Department of Far Eastern Art, Jean K. Schmitt, Curator and Administrator, Maxwell Hearn, Assistant Curator; Department of American Decorative Arts, Berry B. Tracy, Curator in Charge, Morrison H. Heckscher, Curator, Marilynn Johnson Bordes, Associate Curator; Department of European Sculpture and Decorative Arts, Olga Raggio, Chairman, James Parker, Curator, William Rieder, Associate Curator.

A number of other Metropolitan Museum departments and offices have provided assistance, including the Department of Loans; the Registrar's Office; the Objects Conservation Department, specifically John Canonico, Susan Klim, and Rudolph Colban; the Photograph and Slide Library; and the Photography Studio, whose manager Mark Cooper and photographer Sheldan Collins enabled us to illustrate some of the fine points of cabinetmaking.

I would also like to thank Robert H. Ellsworth for amplifying our understanding of Chinese furniture; John Kaufmann and Pridetan Corporation for providing new leather for the Süe and Mare desk; and Wendell Castle for reupholstering the desk and returning it to its original splendor.

I am pleased to express my thanks on behalf of the Memorial Art Gallery to all the above and especially to Wendell Castle and Penelope Hunter-Stiebel for sharing with all of us, through this exhibition and catalogue, their knowledge of and delight in the fine art of the furniture maker.

Bret Waller
Director
Memorial Art Gallery
of the University of Rochester

Wendell Castle and Penelope Hunter-Stiebel examine a table by Clément Rousseau in a storeroom of The Metropolitan Museum of Art.

INTRODUCTION TO ARTIST AND CURATOR

Top: Wendell Castle in his Scottsville, New York, studio. Middle: Chest of Drawers, 1980, mahogany. Bottom: Zephyr Rocker, 1979, curly maple.

WENDELL CASTLE is one of the best known and highly respected furniture artists in America today. Born in Emporia, Kansas, in 1932, he has his B.F.A. in industrial design and M.F.A. in sculpture from the University of Kansas. He taught at several universities before establishing the Wendell Castle Workshop in 1980 in Scottsville, New York, just outside of Rochester. Located in a restored 1890 bean mill, the Workshop offers a two-year program in woodworking for artist-craftsmen, as well as a variety of short-term workshops. Mr. Castle, who resides in Scottsville with his wife, potter Nancy Jurs, and daughter Alison, has been the recipient of numerous grants and prizes, including a Louis Comfort Tiffany Foundation Grant and several grants from the National Endowment for the Arts. He is the author of the *Wendell Castle Book of Wood Lamination.* His work is represented in a number of major institutions throughout the country and abroad, including the Museum of Modern Art and the American Craft Museum in New York, the Boston Museum of Fine Arts, the Philadelphia Museum of Art, and the Smithsonian Institution, as well as the Memorial Art Gallery of the University of Rochester and The Metropolitan Museum of Art, which provided, respectively, the space and the objects for the exhibition this catalogue accompanies.

Wendell Castle has been experimenting with furniture as a sculptural form for some two decades now, attempting to free wood forms from structural convention, yet not ignoring the plethora of furniture making traditions and techniques of the past. He has an insatiable curiosity about and broad knowledge of not only the fine art of furniture making, which he has adopted as his own, but the history of art in two as well as three dimensions. He is a voracious reader and looker who isn't afraid to say he likes beautiful art; he is a modernist, but he is also a traditionalist. Of his work Mr. Castle has said: "My quest as an artist has been primarily involved with the imaginative transformation of organic form—a quest which was first seriously undertaken in the Art Nouveau period. I'm also interested in giving a piece of furniture a personality, a presence."

PENELOPE HUNTER-STIEBEL is Associate Curator in the Department of Twentieth Century Art at The Metropolitan Museum of Art, where her curatorial responsibility ranges from turn-of-the-century Art Nouveau to the vital Studio Craft Movement of the present—of which Wendell Castle is a leading figure. She holds her B.A. in European history from Barnard College and M.A. from the Institute of Fine Arts at New York University, where, under Pierre Verlet of the Louvre, she specialized in French eighteenth century decorative arts. She joined the Metropolitan in the Department of European Sculpture and Decorative Arts, working with applied arts from the Renaissance to the nineteenth century. In 1971 she installed the first gallery of Twentieth Century Decorative Arts at the Museum. Born in Washington, D.C., in 1946, she is married to the New York art dealer Gerald G. Stiebel and has a son, Hunter, and two stepchildren, Catherine and Daniel.

Mrs. Hunter-Stiebel has written and lectured extensively on the decorative arts and has served as judge at a number of exhibitions and competitions. She is recognized in the contemporary crafts field as a knowledgeable and zealous spokesperson and her acquisition of outstanding modern works—including the metalwork of Albert Paley, the glass of Harvey Littleton, and the furniture of Wendell Castle—has generated interest among other museums and collectors. The Metropolitan's Twentieth Century Decorative Arts Gallery presents a changing panorama of decorative arts from the late nineteenth century to the present, presided over by the huge Art Déco mural from the Grand Salon of the ocean liner *Normandie* and an Art Moderne elevator rescued from a building in Rockefeller Center.

Penelope Hunter-Stiebel in the Metropolitan's Twentieth Century Decorative Arts Gallery.

French Panel
Baroque, c. 1680
Oak
H. 73-1/4, W. 40-3/4
Metropolitan Museum of Art
Purchase, Rogers Fund, 1905

LOUIS XIV PANEL

PHS: This oak panel was carved in the period of Louis XIV, around 1680.

WC: The moldings are so clean—they look as if they're almost brand-new.

PHS: They are fairly new, as a matter of fact, because the panel has been reframed. What you're seeing now are only sections of the original piece, which was probably a door. It's a good example of the full-blown Baroque style.

WC: It doesn't really look very Baroque—at least what I think of as Baroque.

PHS: In the French Baroque period there's a great emphasis on volume, not just a dull repetition of classical motifs. It's a very refined, stately style.

WC: There's a lot of depth to the carving. You can see the carver was working with a thick piece of wood.

PHS: The wood was not intended to be exposed as it is now. Most likely it was covered with a protective layer of gesso, then paint, and finally parts would have been topped off with a layer of gold leaf.

WC: It's fared better than other pieces that have been gessoed, where the detail doesn't appear in the carving itself, but in the gessoing. This panel is cleanly cut—the detail is in the wood. There are a few sections on it that look like errors, but I guess the carver wouldn't be very concerned about them, because they could just be covered up with gesso. Oak's an odd choice for the wood, though, because it's so hard to carve. A lot of carving—in England, for instance—was done in other, softer woods.

PHS: Most of the paneling of this period in France *was* oak.

WC: What kind of a room would this have been in?

PHS: It must have been made for a state apartment in a royal residence or official building, because one of the two other panels in the collection that form a set with this one have royal emblems.

WC: Where do you think the design for something like this came from? Would the carver himself have thought it up?

PHS: An *ornemaniste,* or designer of decorations, could have originated the motifs, but the architect would have been responsible for the construction project. Most likely he would have visited the workshop while the panel was being made because he always had to be on top of his commissions.

WC: In England they didn't seem to have it as well regulated. There must have been more control over the ornament in France.

PHS: Exactly. There was a lot more control over everything. Essentially, Louis XIV made the arts state-run. There was an official style defined by a court-appointed *ornemaniste*.

WC: English carvers apparently were on their own. They collected pattern books, looked at them, and then were given several yards of molding to carve. I get the impression they weren't handed a complete project very often.

PHS: There was no improvising here—this was all drawn up on paper and the woodworker had to follow that drawing.

WC: A carver had to be very skillful to do this type of work. A drawing wouldn't tell you all that much about how to carve these flowers, for example. It wouldn't tell you the dimensions or how high to make the relief. All that had to be done by a special carver with a good understanding of just how flowers were carved. This is probably the work of several people—a master and a couple of apprentices, maybe even two masters.

PHS: Yes, there was most likely a master of flower carving, another of military emblems.

WC: Is there a lot of symbolic meaning to the objects represented—the arrows, the helmet, the sword?

PHS: It is standard classical symbolism for war or, rather, military might, something the French cared very much about.

WC: What's amazing to me is the amount of carving that must have been done in those days. Any one of these panels is great, but they had miles and miles of them.

PHS: True, but this represents the top quality of what was being done.

WC: Yes, I think so, too. Today the skill to do this is virtually lost.

PHS: It's strange to imagine how it must have looked originally. In 1680 it was meant to be as splendid in its surface—in its gold and white—as it was in its carving. The things we enjoy now, like the grain of the wood, were not particularly appreciated back then. They wanted it to be dazzling and glittering.

WC: Was gessoing a separate art or was it part of the gilding process?

PHS: The *repareur* did the gesso work, laying the base for the gilder.

WC: I can't imagine how they applied both the gesso and the gold leaf onto those hard-to-reach carved spots.

PHS: The whole purpose of such a piece was to create the effect

Louis XIV wanted, to strike awe in the hearts of his subjects and foreigners, and to have it say "This is the glory of France."

WC: It's wonderful that a piece like this is still around for us to appreciate. There have got to be as many man-hours of work in it as there are in a tract house today. And this is far more valuable!

LOUIS XV PANEL

PHS: There's a real evolution in style here from the earlier panel, going from Baroque to Rococo, from the 1680s to the 1740s. This walnut panel was carved in the reign of Louis XV. There's more gaiety and humor in it and more freedom for the carver, too. Here you've got a representation of hunting—the dog with his prey at the top—and one of fishing—the treasures of the sea at center. The figures on either side could very well represent Asia and Europe.

WC: I see one figure lost his arm, the other his foot. That's probably because the piece was so fragile. Actually, it's amazing more of this hasn't broken off. The carvers never seem to do quite as well with the people. They're like an amateur's attempt at figures. But the other sections of the panel are so incredibly fluid—the bird and the dog are very finely carved.

PHS: And the fish is wonderful, with its bared teeth.

WC: Do you think this would have been gilded, too?

PHS: Either that or painted.

WC: But it's walnut. Why did they have to use a fine wood like walnut if they were just going to cover it up?

PHS: Good question. But there weren't many pieces left in their natural state in the Louis XV period, although we have no documentation on the piece to know exactly how it appeared. It was the fashion in the nineteenth century to strip everything down, so we usually assume that paneling of this or any earlier period found today has been stripped. A piece like this begs for color, it's a cheerful, lively subject. The coins just *had* to have been gold. The color schemes in a room, including the upholstery, were quite marvelous and tended to convey gaiety. The walls didn't always have to be white and gold, either; they could be a combination of any pastel color and white, or polychromed.

French Panel
Rococo, c. 1740
Walnut
H. 102, W. 56
Metropolitan Museum of Art
Gift of J. Pierpont Morgan, 1906

Detail at right

WC: They could heighten the realism of the carving with painting, too. There are a couple of pretty big blank areas.

PHS: If the piece had been polychromed, you'd have needed them to help make the whole thing readable. The spaces would have been very important.

WC: This isn't the kind of tour de force some of Grinling Gibbons's works are. It's simple in comparison to his woodwork.

PHS: But Grinling Gibbons created a name and fame for himself and he was the only one that did. It wasn't by accident, it was because his work was really unique. This panel is very good work of its kind, but it just isn't an independent artistic expression. It was conceived as part of an ensemble, unlike the Gibbons staircase in the Metropolitan's collection, which is an entity unto itself.

WC: I think this is all carved out of one piece of wood, although the carvers in that period weren't beyond adding pieces if necessary. Sometimes they'd go through the wood and have to make a patch. But the primary intention was to get the composition out of the wood they started with. They might have had a carpenter or joiner to get the pieces of wood ready for carving. The carpenter would have been one of a team of people who would have turned it into a panel.

PHS: Yes, because this had to be fitted together with other decorative panels and structural carpentry to make a complete room.

LOUIS XVI PANEL

PHS: Now we have a real change in taste, from the Rococo to the Neoclassical style. The early French Neoclassicism, before Napoleon, is almost feminine in its delicacy and miniaturism, and this Louis XVI panel, from 1784, is a prime example of it.

WC: And it was hung up like a painting?

PHS: Yes, the focus is a new and different one. It's no longer an architectural member or a background. This is an object to be looked at and admired, for its technique as well as for its design.

WC: In this case the carver himself probably did the design.

PHS: Yes, and we know his name: It's signed by Aubert Parent. So you're getting closer to the Grinling Gibbons ethos.

WC: Is there anything known about this artist's other works?

PHS: Yes, it seemed that still lifes like this were Parent's specialty. He was a wood sculptor and architect who showed in the Salons of the late eighteenth and early nineteenth centuries.

WC: He surely was good—I could study this for hours. And there wouldn't have been any gilding on it?

PHS: No, this is plain, beautiful woodwork.

WC: He's used a piece of fine wood as well, a fruitwood. Is the frame original?

PHS: No, and I really don't know what kind of frame it would have had originally. Here you've got a combination of incredible realism—the flowers—and the resurgence of Neoclassicism—the relief of Charity.

WC: Everything is cut so cleanly, nothing is sanded. There might be some scraping to get that polished background surface.

PHS: And the relief can get so shallow, like those leaves on the extremities of the composition.

WC: You've got funny scale relationships, too. The birds, for instance, aren't in scale with the flowers. It's very hard for me to think of one composition having high relief and low relief and objects on different scales. I always imagine things being uniform in a single composition.

PHS: That insect on the leaf is amazing, with its tiny legs, even its knee joints.

WC: Now that is *really* hard to do. Was that an attempt at humor?

PHS: I doubt it. You've got the various symbols of charity, from the bird family to the mythological metaphor of Charity on the plaque—the mother feeding her children. Man and Nature are represented as parallel. It was all done on quite a serious level.

WC: The feathers look absolutely real, but it's not the same kind of realism as in the leaves next to the birds. If you're up close you can see all the chisel marks, whereas on the birds there are no marks. I don't understand how anybody could get back underneath and carve those flowers.

PHS: Do you think they might have been attached afterwards?

WC: No, they were all carved out directly on the piece. I don't think the carver was into any easy way out. They also had a lot of tools then that we don't have today.

PHS: Really, they had *more* tools? How can tools have been lost?

WC: They had access to a blacksmith who made a special tool

French Panel
Neoclassical, 1784
Aubert Parent (1753-1835)
Lime wood
H. 37-1/2, W. 30-1/2 (with frame)
Metropolitan Museum of Art
Gift of Mr. and Mrs. Charles
Wrightsman, 1971

Detail above

for a special job. A master carver—by the time he got to be a master carver—may have had about 300 tools. There probably aren't more than thirty different tools you can buy today. You can buy different sizes of the same tool, but there aren't more than thirty kinds.

PHS: And you can't have them made up?

WC: You could, but they'd be difficult and costly to make.

PHS: It's amazing that there's one field in which the eighteenth century was more technologically advanced than the twentieth!

CHINESE CHAIR

Chinese Chair
Ming Dynasty, c. 1575-1600
Southeast Asian rosewood
H. 45-5/8, W. 23-1/2, D. 19
Metropolitan Museum of Art
Purchase, Seymour Fund, 1967

PHS: The Museum's files record this chair as early Ch'ing Dynasty—around 1700—but it has recently been thought to be considerably older, dating from late in the Ming Dynasty, around 1575 to 1600. Apparently some chairs of this form exist without the extra slat under the arm. I wonder if there's any particular reason for it.

WC: Structurally there is. If the arms were straight the stress would be equal, but these are curved, so without the slat there would be an uneven stress on the join. On straight arms it would be unnecessary.

PHS: I notice that there are traces of some sort of mount at the center of the back.

WC: I noticed that, too. There probably was something added later and then taken off. I doubt if it would have been there originally.

PHS: When I was doing research on this chair, I was amazed to find that most books on Chinese art covered painting, ceramics, metal—absolutely everything except furniture. I was trying to get some information about the form of the chair. One of the books said it was a scholar's chair because the shape of the crest rail is in the form of a scholar's hat, but I think that's stretching it a bit. In paintings I've seen, specifically ancestor portraits, the chair is always draped. Apparently that was seasonal: In the winter you'd have a cloth over it and in the summer it would be bare.

WC: Were there any footstools that went with these types of chairs?

PHS: There could be, but there didn't have to be. The foot rail was a support that could have served that purpose, although this one seems too low to rest your feet on.

WC: The seat is so high that they probably used the front slat to get up on it. Obviously they did need and use it, because it's worn.

PHS: It also kept their feet off the cold, damp tile floors. The height gives the chair a throne-like connotation as well.

WC: All these chairs didn't have straw mats—I've seen them made entirely of wood.

PHS: Yes, and those that were all wood often had pillows on them.

WC: I imagine it was the same for chairs in China as it was in

Europe at the time, that you didn't have them unless you were someone of importance, of high social standing or relatively wealthy.

PHS: They seem to have come in sets—in twos, fours, sixes—often with a table to go with them. There was a real sense of symmetry in the way Chinese furniture was arranged. This type of chair could be moved around quite a bit—into the garden, for instance. Its form was first known in China in the eleventh century, yet it looks so modern to our eyes.

WC: They must have been about the first people in history to give the lumbar region of the back support. We didn't get around to that in the West until the twentieth century. It reminds me of Danish furniture of the 1940s and '50s.

PHS: Yes, we have a Danish chair in our collection which is so obviously derived from a Chinese chair. But of course that's not the first adaptation of Chinese furniture in the West—you get Chippendale's *chinoiserie,* with all its references to Oriental pieces.

WC: But those chairs don't have this kind of joinery. These were put together without glue or nails, though I notice traces of glue on it, probably from someone who restored it.

PHS: I have learned that this chair is made of *huang hua-li* wood, which is often translated as Southeast Asian rosewood. It's a type of wood that apparently was harvested to extinction in China in the seventeenth and eighteenth centuries.

WC: The rosewood that we have today is either Brazilian or East Indian, but in seventeenth century China, rosewood could be obtained from India, Southeast Asia, or the Hunan Province of China. It might even have been imported through Arab trading.

PHS: A lot of chairs of this shape don't have this extra bit of ornament in the front, under the hand rest. I wonder if it has any significance?

WC: It could be structural, giving the chair extra support from racking. But I think it's probably decorative.

PHS: What about these additional pieces of wood along the legs and under the seat rail—are they structural?

WC: They're very definitely structural: That's a minor lap joint. It adds a lot of stability because these are very thin members, very thin frets. The chair wouldn't stay together without them. It's a marvelous example of integrating decoration with structure. It's pretty hard to say what's decorative and what's functional, because they're combined so well. In most cases I'd say they're both.

PHS: I think what you're saying about the integration of form and function is really evident in the back splat, which is so sculptural and yet advanced in terms of supporting the person who's sitting in the chair.

WC: Yes, the way it curves is absolutely sensible.

PHS: And it's probably the most beautiful part of the chair.

WC: It's a very nicely proportioned, elegant piece of furniture.

WILLIAM & MARY CABINET

PHS: This cabinet exemplifies the period when the development of palace furniture traditions began in both England and France.

WC: Is this English?

PHS: This *is* English, but it could pass for Dutch. That's not surprising, because at this point in time, around 1700, there had been a great deal of interchange between Holland and England. Charles II had lived in exile in Holland during Cromwell's reign and then, when Mary assumed the throne in 1688, her husband William of Orange came over with his Dutch entourage. There was a massive influx of Dutch workmen and Dutch style into England.

WC: The seaweed marquetry is typically Dutch. Gerreit Jensen made some good examples of it, didn't he?

PHS: Yes, and he was a Dutch cabinetmaker working at the English court. We don't know who made this piece, but it's certainly of the caliber of court furniture. The view of the cabinet with the doors open was meant to be as impressive as that with the doors closed. The point at which furniture becomes a demonstration of status in society is represented in this piece. Owning it was as important as having jeweled buckles on your shoes.

WC: Do you have any idea how they did this marquetry?

PHS: They would glue together two sheets of thin wood, stencil the pattern, cut through the sheets with a fretsaw, and then separate them. Holly and walnut are the woods used for the marquetry here.

WC: I know that technique, but this work seems too fine for that.

PHS: There's also burning done on it, producing a marvelous, shadowy effect.

English Cabinet on Stand
William & Mary period, c. 1700
Deal, oak; marquetry of
walnut and holly
H. 62-3/4, W. 45-3/4, D. 21
Metropolitan Museum of Art
Bequest of Marion E. Cohn, 1966

Overleaf:
Detail of cabinet with
doors opened

WC: That was probably done with hot sand.

PHS: And there's engraving, too.

WC: Would these patterns have come from pattern books?

PHS: Most likely. Pattern books became an important means of disseminating designs in the seventeenth century. The engravings of Jean Bérain were widely circulated and his designs were adapted to furniture, lace, and even flowerbeds. The cabinet-maker here might very well have done variations on a theme that he knew from a pattern book, making it all work out into the shapes he wanted.

WC: The mounts don't seem right somehow. They don't seem to be of the same quality as the rest of the piece. The details aren't very crisp and clean.

PHS: Every period had its blind spots. In this case the focus was the marquetry. It's the same with seventeenth century Italian and German cabinets of the most spectacular workmanship. When it comes down to the hardware on them, the cabinet-makers had no qualms whatsoever about using base metal mounts—that weren't even cast well.

WC: They paid a great deal of attention to surface detail on the inside and outside, but not to the mounts or the bottoms of the drawers. See all the cracks under these bandages at the bottom of the drawer? They got there because the grain is going from back to front. Ideally the grain would go across, from side to side, because then, as the wood expanded and contracted, the gap would be at the back of the drawer, where it wouldn't matter very much.

PHS: There doesn't seem to have been much thought given to the problem. Both types of drawer construction are found in seventeenth and eighteenth century pieces.

WC: The entire piece underneath is oak. I've never understood why, but apparently that's what they used for core wood for high quality furniture back then.

PHS: Oak was the standard carcass wood used in Europe because it was cheap.

WC: But oak's not a good wood. It shrinks a lot more than other woods and it's more difficult to dry. Still, this piece held up pretty well.

PHS: Yes, considering it's nearly 300 years old!

WC: I assume that the veneer is directly on the solid wood, with no crossbanding in between. It's amazing that it stayed together for so long. It's not finished at the top, though. People were probably a little bit shorter then, so they wouldn't have seen it

Dutch Chair
Baroque, c. 1700-1710
Walnut; marquetry of holly,
boxwood, et al.
H. 44-1/2, W. 20-1/2, D. 21-1/2
Metropolitan Museum of Art
Gift of the Martin Foundation,
Inc., 1973

anyway. Still, it's a nicely scaled piece. What do you think its function was? What did they keep in it?

PHS: Curiously, inventories do not record what such cabinets contained. They were showpieces to be put on display in a state room, a public room, for all to see. A tall blue-and-white Delftware vase would have been placed at the center of the stretcher and a whole set of vases would have been grouped on top of the cabinet. The function of this type of furniture was to show the money and taste of its owner.

DUTCH CHAIR

PHS: This chair is contemporary with the William and Mary cabinet, around 1700 to 1710, but this was made in Holland. It's very Baroque in the complications of its silhouette. The back splat kinks every which way.

WC: I wonder how it sits, because it does have a funny-shaped back. They probably weren't too concerned about that anyway, since it looks like a purely decorative object. To put that much work into something just to sit on it doesn't seem worthwhile.

PHS: It looks sturdy enough with those struts.

WC: It is well made—I think it would hold up pretty well. It's basically a solid wood construction. It had to have been set with its back against the wall, because the marquetry is only on the front.

PHS: It's a formal installation piece and its complicated shapes can only be read from the front. In France there was a formal distinction between the *chaise meublante* and the *chaise courante*. The *chaise meublante* was meant to stand against the wall—it was quite heavy—and the *chaise courante* was a light chair that you picked up and put down wherever you wanted to sit.

WC: The shape of the seat is interesting, with all its curves.

PHS: The front seat rail is a good four or five inches thick.

WC: It's just the same as making a chair that's straight—only you're using a thick piece of wood, so you can give it a zig-zag along the way without sacrificing solidity of structure. The construction is quite normal, actually.

PHS: They just added extra width to be able to do the elaboration.

WC: The arch of the stretcher is amazing, the way it jogs up in

French Console Table
Régence, c. 1715-1725
Oak, marble
H. 31-1/2, W. 18-1/2
Metropolitan Museum of Art
Gift of J. Pierpont Morgan, 1906

the middle. They put in as many turns as they could without sacrificing the function, which is to reinforce the legs. I think they made a serious attempt to make it structurally sound. I like the sculptural detail on the lower back, too, the way the uprights bulge out on either side. I'd like to try that myself. It gives you the feeling that the upright is going to jog out, but you couldn't do that because it would weaken the structure. You have to leave some wood in there to have continuity, so they carved away a set-back, like a web. It's logical, even though it looks purely whimsical.

PHS: The Dutch were the first experts in pictorial marquetry. The imagery here is coming straight out of the still life painting of the period, even down to the elaboration of the tulips.

WC: Look at this line of light wood going up the sides of the back.

PHS: There are breaks in it as it turns corners. They're little fillets of wood making up the line of marquetry, not one long piece.

WC: Evidently they didn't know enough to soak the wood. They didn't know how to make wood bend, even though they were so good at marquetry.

RÉGENCE CONSOLE TABLE

PHS: The style of this console table is associated with Jean-Bernard Toro, who was a French sculptor from Toulon. He popularized the use of carved masks like those on the legs.

WC: The profile of the head is really odd.

PHS: The grimacing face, with its horn-like protrusions and twisted beard, is part of the fashion for grotesque imagery in the early eighteenth century. It's in the Régence style, which marks a transition between Baroque and Rococo. The form has lots of movement, but there's still a symmetrical control, a balance.

WC: This is about 300 years old then? 1700?

PHS: A little later than that, maybe 1715 to 1725. You've still got hangovers from the Louis XIV style in the moldings, which are coming from the basic classical vocabulary. These pieces of furniture, which didn't stand up on their own legs, were considered extensions of the wall. The motifs would have corresponded to the carving of the wall paneling.

WC: And there was probably a mirror above it?

PHS: There could very well have been. The part of the table that would have held the most interest in the eighteenth century was not the support but the marble top. Now we have come to value the carving more.

WC: Marble is easy to cut nowadays, but you can't do this carving today.

PHS: Exactly, so the focus has changed.

WC: I think the concept of a console table is an interesting one. I guess there aren't modern versions because people move around too much and don't want hooks in their walls. If you could have a table against the wall, you would have much more freedom in your leg design. It's practical, too. I've seen some enormous things attached to the wall with no leg or just one leg.

PHS: It's essentially a contradiction in terms, a non-supported table. It liberates design from function. Again, we have a piece that has been stripped in the nineteenth century. You can even see some traces of gesso on it. The rough look of the wood is not true to the original.

WC: I think this is an example in which the gilding would have given it a lot more crispness and made it much cleaner.

PHS: Actually, the whole form is coming out of metalwork, because the silver furniture commissioned by Louis XIV for Versailles was the first to use this kind of flowing movement. Even after the silver pieces were melted down, their image remained in the mind's eye of the king's workmen. They were trying to get the same kind of freedom and movement out of the wood. Then they would gild it to make it look like metal, to approximate the richness of the silver pieces.

WC: Were the silver pieces covered with a thin coat of silver?

PHS: No, they were solid, cast silver. So you literally achieved the liquid form, the flow, since the pieces were cast of molten material.

WC: They didn't think of doing it in bronze?

PHS: No, there was no solid bronze furniture. They immediately switched to wood. It had been the standard material anyway. It was radical when Louis XIV commissioned the silver furniture, which was the most extreme example of court furniture ever made. And it was melted down to fill the nation's war coffers, so it didn't last very long. France needed payment on its war debts at that point more than it needed great furniture.

LOUIS XV WRITING TABLE

PHS: This lady's writing table was for penning social notes, not for conducting business. The drawer was made to hold ink, sandbox, and quill, and there's an extra writing surface that pulls out on the side. This is a classic Louis XV piece in the Madame de Pompadour taste. It's a refined Rococo, not an overwhelming one, and the master of this form was Bernard Van Risenburgh. The François Boucher portrait of Madame de Pompadour showing a similar table by Van Risenburgh is as much a portrait of the table as it is of her.

WC: Wasn't she important in the development of the whole style?

PHS: She really became the leader of this style, its tastemaker. This table appears quite modest next to pieces with more gilded mounts, but it has all the refinement of contour characteristic of the type.

WC: Is it oak?

PHS: It has an oak carcass, but it is veneered with other woods. The floral motif on the top is done in *bois de bout*—in English I think it's called end grain.

WC: It's sometimes referred to as oyster veneer, though it is end grain. You slice off strips of wood from branches and put them together. They've cut it into leaf shapes rather than oyster shapes. It's really fragile and often hard to work with.

PHS: Why, will it fracture easily?

WC: Yes, much more easily. I wonder why the table top has the metal lip—is there a reason? So things won't get pushed off the edge?

PHS: Exactly. That's traditional—to have a raised gallery on three sides. But it's only true of the small writing tables, not the large ones. The movement on the sides is quite wonderful, because that bulge is off-center. It's not a normal *bombé* that projects mostly in the middle. It's an asymmetrical bulge that you hardly even notice. You're just aware of the movement of the form. The leg has been carved in six facets to make it seem even more slender. The projecting one is protected by ormolu, or gilt-bronze, mounts, because that's where the veneer was the most vulnerable to being kicked and chipped. For the same reason the feet were covered with gilt-bronze mounts called *sabots,* or shoes.

WC: There's only veneer on the front two sides of the legs—the

Opposite page:
French Writing Table
Rococo, c. 1760
Tulipwood; marquetry of
kingwood, harewood, and satine
H. 27-1/2, W. 24-1/2, D. 16-1/4
Metropolitan Museum of Art
Bequest of Emma A. Sheafer, 1974

The portrait of Madame de
Pompadour at left shows a
writing table in use.

*Portrait of the Marquise
de Pompadour,* 1756
By François Boucher
Bayerische Staatsgemälde-
sammlungen, Alte Pinakothek,
Munich

Detail of French Writing Table: top view

back sides aren't veneered. The back is solid wood.

PHS: In this period they were much more concerned with what met the eye. In the Louis XVI period there began to be an interest in the interiors. But in the reign of Louis XV the facade and the sculptural form were most important. Not only the surface decoration but its tactile form as well.

WC: What about the shape enclosing the floral design on the top? Doesn't that appear a lot in the Rococo period?

PHS: The cartouche shape is the keynote to the whole French Rococo style. The goldsmith and *ornemaniste* Juste-Aurèle Meissonnier designed a whole repertory of these irregular frame shapes, which was published in the 1720s and '30s. The engravings helped establish the Rococo vocabulary. Even though it is a piece many steps removed from the source, the decoration of the top of this table shows Meissonnier's influence.

LOUIS XV CASKET

PHS: This casket is in essence a miniature commode. In the Louis XV period, when the chest of drawers called a commode was developed, the form became one of the fullest expressions of the Rococo style. A fine example is the commode by Jacques Dubois in the Metropolitan's collection. This mini-commode was made to house a musical mechanism and serve as the base for a clock. That's why you've got the cut-out grilles on the front and sides, and the hole on the side grille for the key to wind up the music box. We can precisely date this piece, because the gilt-bronze mounts are stamped with crowned C's, signifying payment of a tax on gilt-bronze in effect from 1745 to 1749. Those dates coincide with the high point of the Rococo style.

WC: Was it common to remodel things from one use to another?

PHS: The idea of salvaging was certainly common in the eighteenth century. They would take a seventeenth century Boulle cabinet and rework it into a Louis XVI commode, preserving the workmanship and the artistry of the original piece. But I don't think this was remodeled in the 1700s; this was probably done in the late nineteenth or early twentieth century.

WC: The mounts are very well done and the engraving on the latticework is of remarkable quality.

French Casket
Rococo, 1745-1749
Kingwood, gilt-bronze
H. 9, W. 19-5/8, D. 9-1/2
Metropolitan Museum of Art
Purchase, Rogers Fund, 1959

PHS: And the cartouche elements are close to the Meissonnier engravings that helped shape the Rococo style.

WC: I wonder why the mount on the front is hinged to the bottom of the casket. It's a strange way of fastening because they usually put screws right through the mounts. Now you can open the top of the casket, but back then you probably took out that one screw on the mount and swung down the front grille to get access to the music box.

PHS: That makes sense. Although the piece has been taken apart completely and put back together, the treatment of the veneer is what you'd expect on an eighteenth century commode—the veneer cut in four sections with the grain radiating from the center.

WC: I think it's a particularly nice piece, especially because of its mounts. Would these have been standard furniture mounts or would they have been made specifically for this piece?

PHS: They were made in multiples that were the basic stock of the gilt-bronze mount maker. A cabinetmaker would go down the street—literally, because all the shops were quite near each other—to the *fondeur-ciseleur* and say "I'm making up a box so big, what do you have in stock that will work?" And then he could have alterations made on the mount. Have it shaped a little, bent a little, have two bits put together and perhaps reworked.

WC: This does have to fit that exact curve on top.

PHS: Yes, so that corner mount might have been specially made. But these side mounts, these cartouches, we know they existed because one sees the same mounts on other pieces.

WC: It would have been smart to make three or four boxes like this at the same time, wouldn't it? Because then you could have all the mounts custom-made at one time. And I'm sure the molds were reusable.

PHS: Absolutely, they were used for years and years. That's one of the problems of dating many gilt-bronze pieces—because the profession of *fondeur-ciseleur* was passed from generation to generation and so was the stock.

WC: Did the mount maker do his modeling in clay or wax?

PHS: The model was done in clay, then a mold was made in plaster. After that a "master" cast was done in bronze from which further molds could be made as needed. It was the job of the *fondeur-ciseleur,* not the cabinetmaker, to cast the mount and do the final chasing on it. You got varying degrees of chasing on a piece and this one has had a lot of finishing.

WC: It's fantastic to get that kind of detail.

PHS: A lot of work was done on this piece after it came out of the mold. On the really good pieces you'll get these variegated surfaces, like the burnishing on the edge of a volute and the stippling of the inner parts of that same line. Pieces of lesser quality can be really gloppy, left pretty much as they came out of the mold. There was a third party involved—the gilder. You'll get varying degrees of thickness on the gilding as well. This is a good thick one and you can see it on the burnished areas. The gilding is missing on the points of wear, where the piece would have been handled.

WC: Is it gold leaf that's applied to the bronze?

PHS: No, this is mercury gilding. Powdered gold was dissolved in solution with mercury, spread on the metal, then heated— vaporizing the mercury and leaving the gold as an even coating on the bronze. The mercury fumes were poisonous, and the process was banned after the French Revolution.

WC: I wonder why it's not done today. With gas masks and proper ventilation, it shouldn't be dangerous. What would the clock that went on top of this piece have looked like?

PHS: The clock would have been a very sculptural piece, made

The commode at right illustrates the form that has been miniaturized in the casket.

Commode, c. 1750-1760
By Jacques Dubois
H. 33-3/8, W. 56-5/16, D. 25-1/16
Metropolitan Museum of Art
Gift of Mr. and Mrs. Charles
Wrightsman, 1972

almost entirely of bronze. There could have been figures or an animal holding up the clock dial, or it could have been a Rococo essay of leaves and branches.

WC: I think this piece is more significant for its bronzework than its cabinetwork.

PHS: Absolutely. Throughout eighteenth century France the glory of the art of furniture making is shared between the cabinetmaker and the bronze maker.

SHERATON DEMILUNE CABINET

PHS: This demilune cabinet is English, in the Sheraton style.

WC: What's the date on this, approximately?

PHS: It's about 1780. Sheraton-style is just a generic term. Sheraton, Hepplewhite, Chippendale—all were big names because of their published books of models for furniture. The cabinetmakers improvised from there. All the urns, the half-circles, and the other geometry on the piece represent a more academic kind of Neoclassicism than that of the Louis XVI style.

WC: There are half-circles in the front, on the top, and in the overall shape.

PHS: Yes, it's a serious essay on the half-circle. And there's very beautiful marquetry that's enhanced by staining and quillwork, or pen engraving, a feature you wouldn't find on French marquetry. But then there's a nasty little metal knob. The quality falls off terribly with the mounts, just as in the William and Mary cabinet we looked at earlier. Originally there must have been a lot of polychrome stain.

WC: There must have been bright green where you can see the pale green now. Green doesn't stay very well—no color does, really. For some reason the wood always goes back to brown.

PHS: Yes, wood finds its own color again. We do have one French piece in our collection that has some of the original polychromy on it, because they used stained animal horn and mother-of-pearl in addition to wood. The wood's faded out, but you still get some sense of the original colors.

WC: The top hangs over about three inches at the back, which is strange. Maybe it's got the wrong top on it.

PHS: It's one of a pair and they're both built the same way, so it's not an accident.

English Demilune Cabinet
Sheraton style, c. 1780
Spruce, oak, mahogany;
marquetry of satinwood,
partridge wood, and mahogany
H. 36, W. 27-3/4, D. 16
Metropolitan Museum of Art
Bequest of Bernard M.
Baruch, 1965

WC: They were probably built in. They could have been in a place that had a special wall and a jog that fit over something.
PHS: They must have covered the molding line of a dado paneling. The pie wedge drawers spring open from the center on pivot pins.
WC: It's a clever design. There seems to be some secret mechanism that locks from below, so that when one drawer is open, the other is locked.
PHS: That sliding tambour door is a sophisticated bit of cabinetwork.
WC: This is a particularly nice one because you don't realize it's a tambour. It fits so perfectly. The strips of wood are held together by a piece of canvas in the back, I would assume. Because as it goes back there's not enough room for it to store itself, so it has to roll in across the back.
PHS: Is there a pole there that it winds around?
WC: No, a track. The track is laid at the top and bottom. The radius on the track will tighten at the corner so it rolls around behind. It has a false back inside so you don't ever see it. It's a very good job. What kind of finish would have been on this originally? This isn't the original finish, obviously. They had some kind of varnish on it.
PHS: I presume the surface would have been fairly shiny and slick.
WC: French polishing could have been done on this piece. It didn't take any special equipment.
PHS: What is it exactly, just layers and layers of polish?
WC: Layers and layers rubbed on, one at a time. It's very time-consuming. You have to rub it for just the right amount of time, with just the right amount of pressure. Hardly anybody does it today. Hardly anybody *needs* to, because spray finishing gives you a similar look. But a good finish is important for protecting a piece. You need to seal it so that water won't get at it and ruin it and so climate won't affect it as much. I'm sure they put a good finish on this cabinet, even on the back side, although there doesn't appear to be anything on the back of this.
PHS: I've never seen any backs finished that way. I've seen them raw or painted black.
WC: Normally—at least what we accept as the right way to do things today—if you put a finish on one side of a board, you've got to put a finish on the other side. It doesn't have to be the same finish, but some kind of finish, because it's in the

**Details of Demilune Cabinet:
Above, top; right, with
drawers and door opened**

hygroscopic nature of wood that if humidity is going to affect it on one side and not on the other, then it's going to warp. So you want the humidity to go out of both sides of the board equally.

PHS: But that was never done in pieces like this.

WC: I know. If you look at these drawers, for example, they don't have any finish on the back side. So the question is, why didn't they warp? The only thing they had going for them was no central heating. It's hard to believe that makes that much difference, but apparently it does.

PHS: Also, in northern Europe you don't have such wild extremes of humidity as in the United States. Moreover, in the eighteenth century cabinetmakers were interested in making and selling as much furniture as possible. Their concern was how a piece looked the day it left the workshop, not how it would age.

EMPIRE MEDAL CABINET

Drawing for
Empire Medal Cabinet
By Charles Percier
Musée des Arts Décoratifs,
Paris

PHS: This medal cabinet was long thought to have belonged to Napoleon, but as with so many things associated with the Emperor, recent scholarship has disproved this. It is recorded in the sale of the collection of the artist Vivant Denon on his death in 1826. Baron Denon was indeed a friend of Napoleon's and even accompanied him on the Egyptian campaign.

WC: I think the bees are wonderful. What's the reason for them?

PHS: Napoleon adopted the bee to replace the royal emblems of the fleur-de-lis and the intertwined L's.

WC: This has a finish all around it, unlike the Sheraton cabinet we were looking at. Of course, the workmanship on this piece is finer on the whole. The drawers are all on tracks.

PHS: Each drawer is numbered on a silver plaque on its top edge. There are forty-four in all, twenty-two of graduated size on each side.

WC: Who did the engraving on the silver?

PHS: Biennais did all the metalwork, including the amazing hinged wings on the bees that flip out to make drawer pulls. The doors only open when a key is inserted in the keyholes concealed behind the bodies of the serpents, where Biennais discreetly hid his signature.

WC: I responded to this piece because of its overall shape. It's a simple, monolithic form. It looks very contemporary.

PHS: The form is actually a pylon, the one at Ghoos that Vivant Denon illustrated in the journal of his travels through Egypt. There is a working drawing attributed to Charles Percier, Napoleon's official *ornemaniste,* that transforms the romantic ruin into a piece of furniture. It is in the Paris Musée des Arts Décoratifs, among the papers from Biennais' atelier.

WC: This is certainly a very clean, straightforward piece, in spite of all the metal on it. They didn't have any way to glue the silver on, so it's set in with tiny pins. It's an incredible fitting, really. It's hard enough to have to fit something on one plane, but to have to make this banding going around all the moldings is very difficult. There are problems and inconsistencies in the woodworking. It seems as if they intended to have floating panels, allowing the sides to expand and contract, but somehow they got stuck and cracked. Maybe it was done by someone who wasn't sure whether he was a joiner or an *ébéniste.*

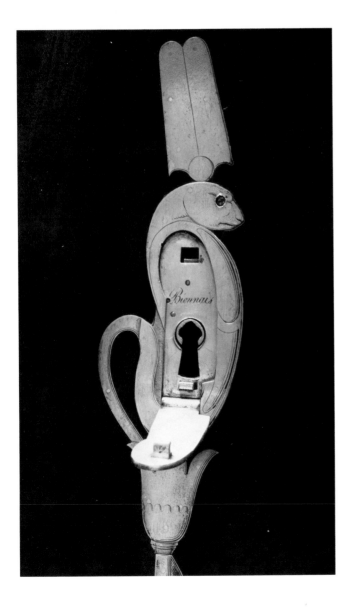

French Medal Cabinet
Empire period, c. 1805
Designed by Charles Percier
(1764-1838); mounts by
Martin-Guillaume Biennais
(1764-1843)
Mahogany, silver
H. 35-1/2, W. 19-3/4, D. 14-3/4
Metropolitan Museum of Art
Bequest of Collis P.
Huntington, 1926

Details, silver drawer pull
and concealed keyhole

PHS: The cabinetwork has been attributed to Jacob-Desmalter because Vivant Denon owned a bed and chairs in the Egyptian style by him. He was a second-generation furniture maker. His father Georges Jacob was a leading *menuisier* of the Louis XVI regime who specialized in chairs. Although he was a top official of the guild during the Revolution, he participated in the dissolution of the system. He then entered the field of *ébénisterie,* as did his sons later.

WC: The cabinetmaker was in a transition period between two ways of working and I'm afraid he used a little of both techniques. Which would have been the smart way to do it, but it wasn't done quite right.

PHS: There is another possibility. The entire cabinet could have been done by Biennais. His is the only signature on the piece and we know he supplied wood boxes with elaborate fittings to contain his works in silver. This piece entailed working to a larger scale than he would have been accustomed. That might explain why there is such finesse in the little drawers and the hinging, while there are problems with the large wood panels.

WC: It's the kind of cabinet that doesn't look like a cabinet. It could be a mahogany sculpture base or a plinth.

PHS: It weighs a ton—maybe all the medals are locked up on the other side!

WC: How does a piece like this end up over in this country? I wouldn't think the French government would let it out. I'd think they'd want to keep it for themselves.

PHS: That would certainly be the case today, but this has been here for a while, since 1926. It was only after World War II that the regulation of the movement of art became an issue of nationalist politics.

English Settee, c. 1885
Designed by Sir Lawrence Alma-Tadema (1836-1912); executed by Johnstone, Norman & Company, London
Ebony, boxwood, sandalwood, ivory, mother-of-pearl
H. 36, L. 57, D. 28
Metropolitan Museum of Art
Bequest of Elizabeth Love Godwin, 1975

Side view

ALMA-TADEMA SETTEE

PHS: This settee was part of the furnishings for the Music Room of Henry Marquand's house in New York. The whole room was commissioned from the painter Sir Lawrence Alma-Tadema. The ceiling was by Frederick Leighton and Edward Poynter did the painting above the keyboard of the grand piano. The Steinway was the focal point of the room, but Alma-Tadema provided the room's overall design. It's a kind of fantasy on a classical theme,

Piano and Stools, c. 1885
From the Marquand Music Room
Designed by Sir Lawrence
Alma-Tadema
Private collection

which is exactly what Alma-Tadema's paintings were. But there's no classical piece we can point to in Greek or Roman history that looked anything like this.

WC: He had pieces of furniture in many of his paintings—were they all made up as much as this piece? Or were some of those a little more authentic?

PHS: They are usually imaginative, but they don't present such a bravura elaboration of techniques. The London firm of Johnstone, Norman & Company made this furniture. We know very little about them. They couldn't have had many grand commissions like this, but they certainly succeeded in combining a number of materials and a variety of techniques.

WC: It's pretty fine workmanship.

PHS: There was a lot of interest recorded in the press in 1885, when the pieces were exhibited in London before being sent to

New York. The Alma-Tadema furniture can be compared to the
Herter Brothers table for the Vanderbilt mansion. They were
both made in that Beaux-Arts moment, when artists were into
raping the history of ornament and combining into a single
entity all the elements they could make off with. Unlike
Vanderbilt's commission, Marquand had his room designed with
a strict overall eye, every piece was coordinated with the next
piece. The same themes occur over and over, because Alma-
Tadema, the number one artist of the day, was responsible for
the total design scheme.

WC: He was the number one artist of his day? I hadn't realized
that.

PHS: Yes, he was one of the very few really rich artists, one of a
small number of artists in history who made it to the top in
wealth, fame, and social status. But then he was forgotten—
fickle history—until almost a century later. To illustrate the
extent of his comeback, the piano that went en suite with this
settee sold for $390,000 in New York in 1980.

WC: Yet all these pieces survived; they didn't go off to the
Salvation Army.

PHS: This piece was bequeathed to the Museum in 1975 by
Marquand's granddaughter; it had stayed in the family all those
years. The piano and the other pieces were bought in the 1920s
by Martin Beck, the theatrical producer. They were on view in
the mezzanine lobby of the Martin Beck Theatre up until a few

English Settee, c. 1885
Designed by Sir Lawrence
Alma-Tadema (1836-1912);
executed by Johnstone,
Norman & Company, London
Ebony, boxwood, sandalwood,
ivory, mother-of-pearl
H. 36, L. 57, D. 28
Metropolitan Museum of Art
Bequest of Elizabeth Love
Godwin, 1975

years ago. At intermission you could sit on the Alma-Tadema chairs, which somehow added to the whole theatrical experience.

WC: The reason I was attracted to this piece in the first place is that I'm attracted to Alma-Tadema's paintings. I don't think I would have given the piece as much attention if it hadn't been associated with him. The front doesn't offer you much, so you might easily miss its best view, which is the side. And you've got to see it close up to appreciate the quality of the workmanship, as well as the design. It's made up of natural history elements, abstract elements, historical elements—everything thrown in together. But they work well as a whole.

PHS: One of the things that unifies the side is the use of the ivory. Your eye tends to follow its strong white lines. There's the right angle, the two curves along the back, and the sort of question mark on the leg that hold the entire thing together.

WC: The technique isn't really remarkable, but it's fine workmanship. The carving and inlay are not as amazing as that on the eighteenth century French pieces. But you don't usually see all of these things together in one piece—the ivory inlay, the marquetry, the carving, and the several different kinds of wood.

PHS: That's so characteristic of the Beaux-Arts period, putting everything together. Would each of these elements have been carved separately before the piece was assembled?

WC: They probably did a pre-assembly and then took it apart.

PHS: So you would have to rough-carve it, then assemble it, then take it apart, and then do the final carving.

WC: Isn't this type of piece unusual for English furniture?

PHS: In a sense you have an international style in high nineteenth century art and this piece is a marvelous document of its period. It's Crystal Palace-type work, showing a multiplicity of techniques and ornament. One usually associates that sort of thing with the Continent, not Victorian England, but the English obviously had the technology, the techniques, and the craftsmen to do it—this piece proves it.

WC: One thing that bothers me about it is that it's too long, like an extrusion. I think it would look better as a chair, since it's the two ends that are important.

PHS: The stripes of the replacement upholstery are upsetting, too. They interfere with the piece's architectonic elements, which would have matched the moldings in the room. The original upholstery was probably the subtle, dull green fabric woven with a pattern of small palmettes that we found on the back of this piece. Its subdued Neoclassicism would have blended in very well.

WC: This isn't done in any particular style, is it?

PHS: The style is historicism. But you're talking about historicism with all the stops pulled out.

HERTER BROTHERS TABLE

PHS: The date on this Herter Brothers table is early 1880s. It existed in the same type of Beaux-Arts context as the Alma-Tadema settee, only it was created for the library of William Vanderbilt's Fifth Avenue mansion. Illustrations of that room show an incredible multiplication of ornament: walls hung with fabrics, lots of upholstery with lots of cushions and tassels, just elaboration upon elaboration.

WC: I see the fragile bits have had a problem here. Quite a bit of inlay is missing in spots.

PHS: Yes, this piece has had a very hard life. Whereas the Tobey and Alma-Tadema furniture remained in the families of their original owners, this has been all over the place. But considering the elaboration of the table, the condition isn't that bad. This inlay along the side of the top corresponded to the molding and inlays throughout the room, along the walls and on the mantelpiece. But the final effect wasn't one of unity in that room; it was more an essay on multiplicity. The whole

American Library Table, 1882
Herter Brothers, New York
Rosewood, brass, mother-of-pearl
H. 31-1/4, L. 60, W. 35-3/4
Metropolitan Museum of Art
Purchase, Gift of Mrs. Russell
Sage, by exchange, 1972

Side view

thing was supposed to look Neoclassical.

WC: It doesn't look very Neoclassical to me, except for the paw feet and the volutes. The brass inlay is very well done, although I don't understand how they worked with it.

PHS: Look at the overlaps in the ribbons on the inlay at the side of the top. The ribbon goes under the crossbanding and then over it. It seems to be hammered into a channel.

WC: These aren't just pieces of wire, because they're of different thicknesses. You have to fabricate all the brass, scribe it off, and saw the wood out to fit it. And it's hard to glue these bits in. They didn't have epoxy in the 1880s, so how did so much of it manage to remain intact? It's a thick veneer of rosewood, so the channel is in the veneer. The big difficulty with the inlay is that you've got the metal, the wood, and the mother-of-pearl. You've got three different materials and you've got to sand them all down smooth. They all don't sand at the same speed, however. The wood cuts so much faster. And since this is veneer, you can't sand it down too much or you'll go right through. That's why I'd stay away from putting on three different types of materials myself.

PHS: Do you need that metal surround on the mother-of-pearl?

WC: No, you don't. You see mother-of-pearl work done nowadays on guitars, and it's almost never surrounded by metal. Especially a metal like brass, which is pretty hard to cut. The brasswork is what I can't figure out on this piece. I suppose a jeweler must have fabricated all these bits of metal.

PHS: It's supposedly a design of Christian Herter himself. He must have known the capability of one of his employees who could do this amazing brasswork and pushed him as far as he could go.

WC: Are there more pieces with brass? I've never seen such brasswork. You get simple inlay, but not work like this.

PHS: You get stringing, but not actual imagery in brass, even down to making the crinkles in the ribbon on the wreath.

WC: I know one thing: I wouldn't make this piece for $100,000. Even at the highest possible hourly rate you wouldn't make out very well.

PHS: Herter Brothers were really geared up for this kind of work.

WC: By that point they had some mechanization to help out with certain aspects of furniture making. They might have had machines to do some of the carving. A machine wouldn't do the quality of carving that's on the sides, but it would rough things

American Library Table, 1882
Herter Brothers, New York
Rosewood, brass, mother-of-pearl
H. 31-1/4, L. 60, W. 35-3/4
Metropolitan Museum of Art
Purchase, Gift of Mrs. Russell
Sage, by exchange, 1972

out for you. They've added another leg to take the strain off the real leg, I notice. There's a weak foot that's been broken. But it's a strange design that I really can't relate to very well.

PHS: It's that same Beaux-Arts period, where they didn't do much selection, just kept adding on. I think what detracts from it are jarring elements like the heavy shelf with its boring palmette molding.

WC: That detail looks hackneyed too. It's the kind of thing you get on cheap furniture. I'd be willing to bet the shelf was one of their standard pieces done by a carpenter. It was just adapted to the table.

PHS: Yes. I've seen that so many times on pseudo-Renaissance library tables made in this period. We're back to nasty mounts again, too. We've outgrown the eighteenth century sculptural mounts and we're back to the crude pull.

The library of William H. Vanderbilt's New York mansion, illustrated in *Artistic Houses,* 1883. The Herter Brothers table can be seen at right.

WC: That's probably a standard mount too.

PHS: I think it's the inlay that's so marvelous on this piece.

WC: It's so dazzling; you can't believe it could be done. The mother-of-pearl on the drawers is so attractive, and I like the stars on the top.

PHS: I'm sure that in that very dark library, overhung with drapes, it must have been one of the few spots of light.

WC: The carving isn't very three-dimensional. It doesn't go very deep; it's all rather flat. But it's cleanly done.

PHS: It's absolutely rigid and regular—for instance, the mock-fringe, which is so stick-like, or the paw feet, which are schematized compared to those on the Alma-Tadema settee.

WC: I don't think the carver of this particular piece was very distinguished. The overall workmanship is pretty high, though.

PHS: Originally it was thought that the table couldn't be American because the workmanship was too fine.

WC: It's very nice underneath, too. You don't see screws or un-finished spots.

PHS: In contrast to the Tobey table, where you see all its mechanism.

WC: That's just the difference in the prices that were paid for them.

PHS: I'll bet there was a *big* difference. Vanderbilt's home was really the last word in luxury and artistic decoration in its time.

TOBEY TABLE

PHS: The maker of this table, the Tobey Furniture Company of Chicago, didn't have any great aspirations. They were manu-facturing Arts and Crafts furniture initially—just the simplest oak forms. In the late 1880s they started an art furniture line, of which this table is an example.

WC: By those standards, then, they're using expensive material, even though it's just cherrywood. The quality of the carving is quite good. It's the first piece of furniture that we've seen with solid wood construction on the top, too. Nothing we've looked at up until this showed the wood in its natural state. European furniture would never look like this.

PHS: One of the most interesting aspects of this piece is its architectonic quality. The history of the table isn't quite clear, but its design may be attributable to Louis Sullivan. It probably came out of a Sullivan house that was later bought by the Borden family. We know the table passed through successive generations of the Borden family. Its ornament certainly has a lot in common with the kinds of decoration that Sullivan was using on his buildings in the 1880s. We have chairs to go with it as well, but they're rather ordinary. The table is the strongest piece.

WC: It opens to an enormous size.

PHS: Yes, you can keep adding leaves, and it goes on and on. That's why you have that massive central pillar. You need it for support. The table is really built more like a small building than a piece of furniture.

WC: It's all solid wood—even the stretchers are laminated, there's nothing veneered.

PHS: Are these little leaves on the upper section of the stretchers applied?

WC: Yes, those are applied, but the rest of it is carved from a block. It's hard to believe, but each leg is a solid block of wood.

PHS: There's no attempt to cover up the act of carving either. You really see the marks.

WC: But that's sort of nice and straightforward, to leave the chisel marks. This piece is straightforwardness all over. Compared to European furniture, there's no attempt to hide anything, no attempt to hide the joinery, no attempt to hide any end grain with veneer. They selected the wood fairly carefully except for the top, which is disappointing since the boards aren't matched. Maybe it always had a tablecloth on it.

PHS: I hope it was a tablecloth that didn't hang over too far, or you lose all the decoration—all that for nothing! The honesty of the piece is perfectly in character with the situation, with the Arts and Crafts style of the time. The natural point of departure for the maker was straightforward, honest furniture, which he made a little more imposing and monumental to reflect the architecture of the time.

WC: I would imagine by some of the standards of the time it was considered very plain, simple, and more or less *un*decorated. In comparison to, say, the Alma-Tadema settee or the Herter Brothers table.

PHS: But you have to realize that this was not for a New York City mansion, like those two pieces were, but for a Chicago home. So you've got the whole Midwestern ethos, which leans toward the good and true and simple.

American Dining Table,
c. 1888-1890
Tobey Furniture Company,
Chicago
Cherrywood
H. 29-9/16, W. 53-3/4
Metropolitan Museum of Art
Gift of Mrs. Frank W.
McCabe, 1968

American Side Chair, c. 1880
Attributed to Herter
Brothers, New York
Rosewood
H. 31-1/2, W. 15-3/8, D. 19-1/4
Metropolitan Museum of Art
The Sylmaris Collection,
Gift of George Coe Graves, 1975

HERTER BROTHERS CHAIR

WC: This chair by the Herter Brothers is certainly different from their table we looked at. How did they get from the grand Vanderbilt style to such simplicity?

PHS: This is an example of the new wave of *japonisme* that was coming in from England. The source was William Watt's catalogue of Anglo-Japanese furniture designs by Edward Godwin.

WC: So this is later than Godwin?

PHS: Yes, because Godwin—who was an avid collector of Japanese art—was doing this as early as the 1860s. The catalogue was published in 1877 and the designs got picked up in America a bit later; this chair dates around 1880.

WC: It's not as well-structured as Oriental furniture.

PHS: The simplified fretwork is orientalizing, but not as well made as that on an Oriental chair.

WC: It's an elegant looking chair, but it just isn't sensible design. Godwin's chairs weren't either. They were all skinny legs. This pseudo-stretcher takes a roundabout way of getting from one end to the other—and loses its strength along the way.

PHS: Yes, it loses its support function, because the horizontal is interrupted by the vertical.

WC: But it's nicely proportioned and I imagine it sits fine.

PHS: What the Herter Brothers were doing with this chair was cleaning up their act. They used only a couple of decorative motifs—for example, the swan's head, which really looks more like a snake's head—not a multitude of ornaments. It's quite different from the orientalizing side chairs they made for the Japanese Parlor of Vanderbilt's mansion. They were gilt-maple extravaganzas with mother-of-pearl inlay and Chinese embroidered upholstery.

WC: A piece like this would look good in a set. A lot of them wouldn't be too busy. Has this been reupholstered?

PHS: Yes. It's rare that you find original upholstery.

WC: They used dowel construction. They're taking a lot of shortcuts with the construction all around. It's not a truly hand-made piece. Was it offered in their catalogue as a standard item?

PHS: I wouldn't think there would be much of a demand for it.

WC: For 1880 this had to be super-modern.

PHS: Yes, but the Aesthetic Movement did strike America hard, and *japonisme* was an important component of that movement. Oscar Wilde's tour of America proved a successful means of spreading the word as well.

WC: Yes, Wilde would have approved of this chair.

The mosaic designs on the Tiffany chair at right resemble the stenciled motifs on the entrance hall walls of the Mark Twain House in Hartford, Connecticut, decorated by Louis Comfort Tiffany & Associated Artists in the early 1880s.

American Arm Chair, 1890-1900
Tiffany Glass & Decorating Company
Ash with inlays of ebony, boxwood, mahogany, and satinwood; marquetry of brass and wood
H. 35-3/8, W. 26-1/4, D. 25-5/8
Metropolitan Museum of Art
Gift of Mr. and Mrs. Georges E. Seligmann, 1964

TIFFANY CHAIR

PHS: This Tiffany chair was made between 1890 and 1900, but the form is a traditional *bergère* in the Louis XVI style. The naturalism of the carving on the top is a typical Tiffany touch—just plant on plant on plant, springing out of the grass.

WC: I think the chair would have a problem if you tipped it; it seems to be a bit top-heavy.

PHS: The crest rails and arm and back braces are catalogued as ash, the wide bands around the marquetry satinwood, the checkerboard ebony and boxwood.

WC: It's not ash—I think the whole piece is satinwood. Nobody would ever had made a fine chair out of ash. It's a very porous wood, even more so than oak. Maybe the frame is ash.

PHS: We don't know whether the wood mosaic decorations were imported from India or whether they were made in America. My guess is that these sheets were imported, because this is such a foreign technique, unlike anything in Western tradition.

WC: I'll bet you're right—I'll bet they bought these pieces and fit them into the chair.

PHS: We do know that Tiffany had much of his carving done in the East. Lockwood de Forest, who was a partner in Tiffany's firm Associated Artists, founded workshops in India that produced ornament as well as furniture.

WC: The mosaic work is so curious. You just can't go placing those little inlay bits between the metal with tweezers. You can *do* it—by cutting off little pieces from a long skinny one and shoving them into the grid—but it would take forever.

PHS: So you'd be working with long pieces of wood, like straws?

WC: Yes, normally that's the way things like this are done. Around the holes of guitars, for instance, they have what's called purfling. It's decorative inlay made up of thin slices of wood taken off of a long strip of wood.

PHS: So you'd have sheets of brass and straws of wood, and you'd slice them both?

WC: I can't imagine how the brasswork was done. The mosaic could be manufactured as all wood, but I don't know how you'd ever get the brass in. It's just so tiny.

PHS: Look, it's broken on the side, with only the metal strips left.

WC: Yes, and somebody's faked in an area on the side where

the original is missing. That's not even inlay, that's painted, probably on a piece of canvas. From a distance, though, it doesn't read too badly, it's just a little fuzzy. But where the big strips are concerned, I'd hate to think how many little spots of wood went into them—millions!

PHS: And that they could use it so extravagantly to cover the back of the chair too!

WC: It must not have been anywhere near as difficult as we're thinking it is. There's no reason to think that this is a $100,000 chair, is there?

PHS: No. Unfortunately, there's no history on the chair.

WC: Who made it, exactly?

PHS: The Tiffany Glass & Decorating Company, which was a decorating firm that came into existence in 1890. It was the new name given to Louis C. Tiffany & Associated Artists. They designed interiors as well as objects, including tiles, lamps, stained-glass windows, and furniture. Associated Artists was responsible for the Moorish entryway of the Mark Twain House in Hartford, Connecticut, for one thing. The stenciled designs on its wooden walls are quite similar to the geometric motifs on this chair.

WC: It's a totally handmade chair then, they weren't producing it in quantity?

PHS: I doubt it, although there is a mate to this chair in the Metropolitan's collection.

WC: They had to have done quite a few or else they wouldn't have bothered to set up a cabinetmaking shop with highly skilled people. There must be other pieces around someplace.

PHS: Unfortunately, we don't really know much about Tiffany furniture. A great deal of attention has been paid to Tiffany glass, but less to the bronzes, and still less to the woodwork.

BUGATTI DESK AND CHAIR

PHS: This Bugatti desk and chair probably date from the early period of his work, from the late 1880s to early 1900.

WC: Do we know who actually made them? Was it Carlo Bugatti himself?

PHS: He had a workshop, employing people who didn't really know how to make furniture. The construction is completely erratic: Within one piece you'll find different methods of doing the same thing.

WC: He didn't really intend anybody to use this furniture, did he?

PHS: It couldn't have lasted more than a couple of months with use. If you make a seat as a vellum drum, it will inevitably break.

WC: What's so amazing is that there was any market for it at all, that anybody would even have taken it home if you *gave* it away. It's so far-out.

PHS: It does play to that taste for Oriental exoticism at the end of the nineteenth century. What you've got is an extension of themes that run through nineteenth century French painting, the exoticism of Delacroix and Gérôme. It's not patterned after actual Eastern furniture, it's the stuff of pure fantasy, an improvisation on Moorish motifs.

WC: That's really a lot of inlay, cutting and piercing, copper and other materials.

PHS: The rope isn't original to the chair. You can see holes where a fringe was attached, extending down along the bottom of the seat back and along the seat rails. These openings on the sides of the desk are so funny—they look like alligator jaws. I always thought we were missing two "teeth" here near the front, but there is an exactly parallel gap on the other side, so it must be intentional—they're the jaws of a very old alligator.

WC: The forms are so unusual. They're not based on existing furniture forms at all. This chair has absolutely no regard for any tradition in terms of structure.

PHS: It does have four legs, but they're not exactly in the right places. The stretcher is more important than the legs.

WC: It's the kind of attitude that you see nowadays with some people experimenting with furniture. But nobody does anything as exotic as this. Certain people, myself included, have looked at furniture and tried to approach it in a non-traditional way, but he's got to have been the first to do it.

PHS: A fair amount of Bugatti's furniture has survived. I can't figure out why, except that the French never throw anything away.

WC: It ended up in France? How did that happen?

PHS: Bugatti moved to France from Italy. He started commuting to Paris, where he obviously had a market, and he finally moved there from Milan in around 1904. We know very little about him, but a good deal more about his children. One son,

Italian Desk and Chair,
c. 1888-1902
Carlo Bugatti (1855-1940)
Walnut, brass, rose metal, vellum
Desk:
H. 29-1/2, W. 23-3/4, D. 22-1/2
Chair:
H. 30, Diam. 17-1/2
Metropolitan Museum of Art
Purchase, Rogers Fund, 1970

Rembrandt Bugatti, was a sculptor of animals. Another son, Ettore, designed the classic Bugatti automobile—the best-known achievement of the family.

WC: Some of the pictures I've seen of whole rooms Bugatti designed are amazing.

PHS: His masterpiece was the Snail Room at the 1902 Turin Exposition. It comprised vellum-covered built-in furniture that just snaked around the room. The chairs were heavier than this, cantilevered, and quite sound structurally.

WC: I see the chair is signed on the top piece of vellum. Is this design on the desk any kind of language?

PHS: No, it's pseudo-calligraphic gibberish, just as the roundels are pseudo-Moorish. Apparently the calligraphic pictorial inlays were done by pouring hot metal—pewter, I think—into carved-out channels and then scraping it off. You can even see the scrape marks.

WC: I doubt if it's pewter; it's probably rose metal, which has a very low melting point, about 95° C., much lower than pewter. Did Bugatti give detailed drawings to his workers or did he just come in and give orders?

PHS: We don't know anything about how he worked. We know very little about what he did and who his clients were.

WC: He would have had to have done drawings, because the workmen couldn't have been left at their own discretion to come up with these kinds of things!

PHS: Bugatti might have had the workmen make up elements in numbers, so there might have been a repertory of things out of which he'd take pieces and then construct in an assemblage manner.

WC: It almost looks that way. There may be an Italian tradition for that, as a matter of fact, because there were two Romans—Fabio De Sanctis and Ugo Sterpini—who worked in a similar way in the early and mid-1960s. They'd get pieces of scrap—from castings or from wood shops—put them together, and make the weirdest furniture. I don't think there's any of it in this country and, unfortunately, they're not working in furniture today.

PHS: How do you work with your assistants—do you give them drawings?

WC: I do, but they're not very detailed. They understand the framework in which I'm working, so they have a feeling for the way I want things. Plus I'm not very far away from them, so I can see what's happening. But my designs don't require as many decisions as something like this.

PHS: Do you make a prototype for your assistants to follow?

WC: That's the easiest situation, because then they know exactly what to do, they have something to refer to. On a three-dimensional piece, especially, the drawings aren't as meaningful. These pieces are two-dimensional, so drawings would be very useful. With reasonable drawing skills you could pass along to your workmen renderings of the side, front, and top views and communicate top quality. Do you think some of this ornament might be traditional?

PHS: No, he just made up the stamped and repoussé motifs. He came up with an infinite variety. Motifs aren't repeated even within the same piece. We've seen other nineteenth century pieces, like the Herter Brothers table and the Alma-Tadema settee, where there were consistent themes, where ornament on the furniture corresponded to decorations of the room.

WC: I think they're two very good examples of Bugatti's work.

PHS: The desk works better, because there's one dominant idea, that curve going from the jaws of the alligator to the ground. So many of the pieces are such assemblages—you almost wonder if there was a preliminary design at all, because they just seem to ramble on, with a little turn here, a little fringe there.

WC: I just can't imagine these pieces in a normal room, being used on an everyday basis. They had to have been considered sculptural.

PHS: They were certainly novelty pieces.

WC: It's almost as if he were a theater designer.

PHS: Yes, his rooms resemble stage sets.

COLONNA TABLE AND CHAIR

PHS: This Edward Colonna chair represents the Parisian Art Nouveau of Samuel Bing. It's a much quieter style than that of Gallé and Majorelle and the Ecole de Nancy. You don't have all the literal floral ornament that's so identifiable as Art Nouveau.

WC: It's a very refined and sensitive piece of furniture. It seems that so many styles at their heights go to extremes—and this is an extreme of refinement. It's very fine carving, also. This wasn't a piece that was produced in any great numbers, was it?

PHS: No, not in vast numbers. These things were sold through

Samuel Bing, who was the definer of the style of Art Nouveau—he gave it its name. He got together the artists that he liked with manufacturers who could execute their designs. He exhibited and sold the works in his Paris gallery called *l'Art Nouveau.* So these were pieces that were conceived as works of decorative art and sold by an art gallery. This was not furniture manufactured in bulk and marketed through trade catalogues. A chair of this model was exhibited in Bing's pavilion in the 1900 Exposition in Paris.

WC: Was it a pretty expensive item?

PHS: Yes, but not Vanderbilt expensive. It was art furniture, but the idea was to make such pieces available to a broader public. They weren't trying to use lots of precious materials and thousands of man-hours of workmanship. The emphasis was on the design.

WC: I wonder why they used this screw at the bottom to connect the two parts of the seat rail? Considering all its other fine qualities, it seems the joiner took a short cut there. Because the carving is really first class. Is that the original upholstery?

PHS: Yes, that's why it's been covered in net to preserve it—even though it *is* in tatters. There was supposed to be a real harmony of the motifs of upholstery and the curving of the back. Not a one-to-one match, but a harmony. The Museum bought the chair in 1926 and, believe it or not, the upholstery's decomposition came about from its sitting up on a shelf. The chair and the Colonna table were actually bought at the most unlikely moment. The Metropolitan had a fund in the 1920s to buy modern decorative arts and the curator, Joseph Breck, went over to Paris and bought the latest in Art Déco. But he was aware that there had been another style that came before, so he tried to find examples of it. He contacted the heirs of Samuel Bing to see if there was anything left of his stock. These two pieces were among the remains. But Art Nouveau wasn't recognized as an important style then. It was Breck's curatorial conscientiousness, his attempt to find predecessors to Art Déco, that led him to it. People didn't begin to pay serious attention to Art Nouveau until the 1960s.

WC: The carving on the table is well done, too.

PHS: Yes, it's quite subtle. Again you're taking an almost standard, conservative form and making it lively with the carving at the corners. You have the same kind of flaring foot as on the chair.

WC: Again, it's very sensitive and well proportioned.

French Side Chair
Art Nouveau, 1899
Edward Colonna (1862-1948)
Palisander wood
H. 35-1/4, W. 16-7/8, D. 15
Metropolitan Museum of Art
Purchase, Edward C. Moore
Jr. Gift, 1926

French Table
Art Nouveau, c. 1899
Edward Colonna (1862-1948)
Palisander wood
H. 28-1/2, L. 39-1/4, W. 23-1/2
Metropolitan Museum of Art,
Purchase, Edward C. Moore
Jr. Gift, 1926

PHS: I think every major museum in Europe has one of these tables in a different wood. This is palisander. They bought them when they were new. This seemed to be a piece that spoke to the curatorial eye in 1900. Everyone said, ''That's beautiful, that's refined, that's the example we should have.'' Not the great, massive Majorelle pieces, the ones we love today. They considered this good taste.

WC: It is. The overdone ones are more curiosity items, more flamboyant.

PHS: But I respond to their flamboyance. Hector Guimard—who was certainly flamboyant—is on the top of most curators' desiderata lists, way above Colonna.

WC: Yes, his pieces are more extreme, more exotic. These are really quiet. When you read about fine Art Déco furniture, it says the makers were hoping to return to the high standards of the eighteenth century. They didn't consider Art Nouveau furniture up to those standards, right?

PHS: Yes, and it was true. In the Art Nouveau period they weren't concerned as much with the workmanship as with the design. However they could get it done, they got it done. Majorelle, for instance, ran a furniture factory. The pieces he did for exhibitions were of extraordinary workmanship, but then those endless dining rooms that were pictured in his sales catalogue were not particularly fine.

WC: But it seems to be of reasonable and sound workmanship.

PHS: Of course in France there was such a strong tradition and nineteenth century workmanship was fabulous, much better than what was being done in England and America.

WC: But why are there always references to going back to eighteenth century workmanship, if the nineteenth century's was as good?

PHS: In the nineteenth century they were using as much technology as possible, taking advantage of whatever mechanization they could. The artists were really upset that they were being caught up in repeating historical forms. That's why they started having salons and establishing schools to upgrade the level of design and workmanship. They weren't pleased with what they were doing, but they weren't pleased with Art Nouveau either.

WC: Yes, that's the impression I get. So there were people who could do the work. What were they doing when the Art Nouveau furniture was being made?

PHS: They were making reproduction furniture. That was where

The dining room of the Paris apartment of Auguste Rateau, designed by Lucien Lévy-Dhurmer and executed from 1910 to 1914, is shown in the period photograph at right.

the market was. Even when Art Nouveau pieces were being done, people with money wanted to furnish their homes with reproductions of eighteenth century furniture.

WC: The quality of the carving in a piece like this table is very good, so the maker must have had some sympathy with the form. If he had just hated it, it's hard to believe that he could have done that good a job.

PHS: I think Bing was the key factor there. He was getting the designs from Colonna and he was finding people who could execute them.

WC: Then Colonna didn't have any direct contact with the cabinetmaker?

PHS: Most likely not. Bing would have been the intermediary. Colonna was not responsible for the product—whether it was furniture, jewelry, or porcelain—once he got the design to Bing.

WC: I think in principle it was a mistake, not having the artists more involved in the actual making of a piece.

PHS: Bing was concerned with cultivating first a style and then an audience for that style. He started out selling Japanese imports, then he began to get involved with the possibilities of contemporary Western work. Bing was interested in creating a *nouvelle vague,* in placing an emphasis on aesthetic values. And those aesthetic values were not just applied to the materials and to the workmanship—they were in the artistry of the conception. And that was what was missing in all the reproduction and adaptation work.

ART NOUVEAU DINING ROOM

PHS: These three pieces are all from an Art Nouveau dining room that was designed by Lucien Lévy-Dhurmer between 1910 and 1914. He was primarily a Symbolist painter, not a furniture designer, so they're not particularly innovative in either their form or structure. It's one of the characteristics of many artist-designers—their objects are pictorial rather than structural. The theme of the room was a wisteria garden. Painted canvases of birds and flowers fit into the wood panelings and the wisteria motif was worked into every element of the furnishings, including the crest rails of the chairs and the leatherwork of their backs.

French Side Chair
From the Art Nouveau Dining
Room, 1910-1914
Designed by Lucien Lévy-
Dhurmer (1865-1953); carved
by Edouard-Louis Collet (1876-?)
Walnut, leather, brass
H. 37-1/4, W. 17, D. 16
Metropolitan Museum of Art
Purchase, Harris Brisbane
Dick Fund, 1966

WC: The upholstery seems to be all stapled together.
PHS: No, it's not staples, it's great big stitches.
WC: It's fortunate that the upholstery survived, because without it you'd certainly lose a lot of this effect.
PHS: You need to have that pendant wisteria in the leather on the back to link up the carving on the crest rails and the legs.
WC: Other Art Nouveau pieces used leather upholstery, too, so it's not that unusual.
PHS: Here the concern was creating a total ensemble—not just making pieces for exhibition or for sale.

French Arm Chair
From the Art Nouveau
Dining Room, 1910-1914
Designed by Lucien Lévy-
Dhurmer (1865-1953); carved
by Edouard-Louis Collet (1876-?)
Walnut, leather, brass
H. 39-5/16, W. 22-1/4, D. 19-1/2
Metropolitan Museum of Art
Purchase, Harris Brisbane
Dick Fund, 1966

Overleaf:
French Dining Table
From the Art Nouveau
Dining Room, 1910-1914
Designed by Lucien Lévy-
Dhurmer (1865-1953); carved
by Edouard-Louis Collet (1876-?)
Walnut, rosewood
H. 28-5/8, L. 51-1/8, W. 66-3/4
Metropolitan Museum of Art
Purchase, Harris Brisbane
Dick Fund, 1966

WC: Does the Metropolitan have the whole room?
PHS: Yes, we've got all the paneling, the table, the chairs, two console tables, two standing lamps, the carpet, the fireplace, the paintings.
WC: Do you hope to put it all together sometime?
PHS: It will require a huge investment of money and time, but in the future we hope to be able to install it in the Museum's Southwest Wing, which has yet to be built.
WC: To be able to tear out that whole interior without destroying it is amazing.

PHS: Ever since the eighteenth century, the French tradition was to make these woodwork walls. They're actually like shells sitting within an architectural space to make separate walls of a room. They were very often ripped out and replaced with newer paneling.

WC: The carving's not as fine as, say, Guimard's.

PHS: Nor is the design.

WC: But I think it's very important as a whole. To preserve all that wood is really incredible.

PHS: This is a case where the sum of the parts is much more interesting than any of the parts separately.

WC: In many ways this would be much easier to live with now than pieces of Guimard or Majorelle, which are so overwhelming. And they tend to make you feel uncomfortable. This is more livable.

PHS: It's not as potent and for that reason it's more domesticated. And it's very attractive, too. The paintings, with their pastel colors, are ravishing. You get a harmonics of prettiness going, rather than the strength and guts of a Guimard or somebody from the Ecole de Nancy.

WC: They're very nicely done. There's nothing shoddy about the workmanship.

PHS: The wood carver was named Edouard Collet. We don't know him in any other context, except for working on another room designed by Lévy-Dhurmer, an office for the same client that commissioned the dining room. The patron's name was Auguste Rateau and he was a member of the Academie des Sciences.

WC: It's quite a big project for one cabinetmaker.

PHS: Yes, there was a lot of work involved. He must have had assistance.

WC: I think the carver had an awfully good understanding of the design concept, because structurally the pieces are very sound. They make sense.

PHS: He was taking a standard structure and just adding ornament to it.

WC: You're right, it's not very extreme. The table top is veneered and just has a little design along the corners.

PHS: When Rateau decided to sell the apartment, the prospective buyer wanted a long-term lease, but he could only get one if he agreed to buy all the furnishings. He didn't really want them, but he bought them. There was no interest in Art Nouveau at that time. Years later he was able to sell the room through one of the leading Paris dealers.

WC: I imagine that when Art Nouveau became unfashionable it was *really* unfashionable.

PHS: Right, like Victorian was just a few years ago. You have so many stories of Tiffany lamps and Tiffany windows that were an embarrassment and were literally thrown out. Nobody would take them.

WC: It's such a shame that almost at the time this room was made Art Nouveau was already over.

PHS: Yes, this was one of its last gasps, the world was on the brink of the modern. There's much more schematization compared to the floral decorations on other Art Nouveau pieces. In fact, there's almost a Cubist breakdown on the flowers. It's definitely modernistic.

SÜE & MARE DESK AND CHAIR

PHS: This desk by Louis Süe and André Mare is a historicizing play on an eighteenth century classic. They've taken the shape of the Louis XV *bureau plat* and at once streamlined and exaggerated it. It's almost a pun, covering it with ebony to symbolize *ébénisterie*. The name of the profession of *ébénisterie* was derived in the seventeenth century from the practice of veneering furniture with ebony.

WC: I like its color scheme, the black and gold. They look very good together.

PHS: It was meant to be the star installation in the Grand Salon of Süe and Mare's pavilion at the 1925 Exposition Internationale des Arts Décoratifs et Industriels Modernes. That government-sponsored World's Fair in Paris presented the new French style to an international public. The term Art Déco has since been coined from the abbreviated title of the Exposition.

WC: I think the desk is one of Süe and Mare's best pieces.

PHS: It's such a clever paraphrase, because they've taken all the elements that would be covered in gilt-bronze on the eighteenth century *bureau plat* and again streamlined and modernized the forms. They've got the mount going all the way from the corner to the foot.

WC: There's no leg—it's all mount.

PHS: Yes, so it's exaggerating what would have been done in

French Desk
Art Déco c. 1925
Designed by Louis Süe
(1875-1968) and André
Mare (1885-1932);
manufactured by Compagnie
des Arts Français, Paris
Ebony, zebrawood, ormolu
H. 30-1/4, L. 61-7/8, D. 32-1/2
Metropolitan Museum of Art
Purchase, Edward C. Moore
Jr. Gift, 1925

Detail of left
drawer, opened

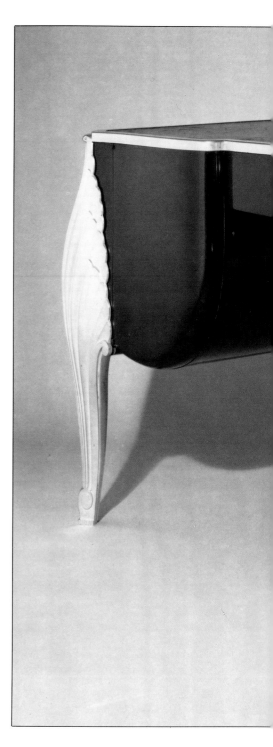

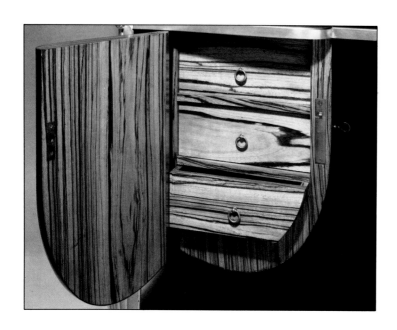

French Chair
Art Déco, c. 1925
Designed by Louis Süe
(1875-1968) and André
Mare (1885-1932);
manufactured by Compagnie
des Arts Français, Paris
Ebony
H. 34-1/4, W. 24, D. 19
Metropolitan Museum of Art
Purchase, Edward C. Moore
Jr. Gift, 1925

Opposite page:
This vintage photograph of
the Grand Salon of the Louis
Süe and André Mare pavilion
at the 1925 Paris Exposition
shows the desk and chair
now in the collection of
the Metropolitan Museum.

the eighteenth century, when the outer edge would have been covered in ormolu, along with the feet and corner mounts. They would never have gone so far as to make a metal leg in the eighteenth century. And you wouldn't have had these low compartments sagging halfway down to the floor, looking so bloated. I think the best part is the veneering—even the underside is veneered.

WC: Is it really ebony? It almost looks too black.

PHS: It's ebony veneer over an ash core.

WC: Nowadays you can't get ebony veneer.

PHS: Where does it come from?

WC: Gaboon ebony comes from Africa, but it's only available in a solid form. You have to get it in a log and make your own veneer. And it's so costly it's sold by the pound.

PHS: The fronts of these bulbous pockets are doors. They open with a key and inside you have a three-drawer compartment veneered with zebrawood.

WC: There's really not a flat surface on it, except for the top.

PHS: It's all bowed—another throwback to the eighteenth century.

WC: This came to the Museum brand-new?

PHS: Yes, it was purchased at the 1925 Exposition.

WC: What's known about Süe and Mare—who did what?

PHS: Neither of them did the actual work himself, that we know. When this piece was made they were heading the *Compagnie des Arts Français,* which was a group of people providing designs and employing artisans to execute them. Both Süe and Mare did furniture designs. André Mare had been a painter and Süe had been trained as an architect.

WC: Süe did some furniture work later by himself.

PHS: Yes, they disbanded the firm in 1928. Mare went back to painting, Süe went on with architecture and furniture design. His later pieces were quite different from these: much simpler, with columnar legs and planar surfaces. But this desk is typical of the style that made Süe and Mare famous in the 1920s. You really see how they were playing off of the Louis XV and Louis XVI styles. They didn't really have originality, that was their main problem. Ruhlmann had originality.

WC: They didn't seem to have a large vocabulary either. They didn't work on expanding it. The desk has a lot going for it, though. The bronze legs, the bulbous surfaces, and the color scheme are very good, but it seems that when they got to the next piece they didn't work on developing their good ideas. Ruhlmann's work seems to have more themes going through it.

PHS: The most original feature of the desk is the stylized wing form that sheathes the leg.

WC: The room that this was in had a similar piano in it, too, didn't it?

PHS: Yes, it had the same legs. They repeated the same motif on the leg, never taking it one step further.

WC: This kind of metalwork just isn't done today. You have metal furniture of tubular steel, but you don't have anyone using eighteenth century ideas on mounts. But I don't think it's that unreasonable. A sculptor ought to be able to do it—it's a modeling job, with wax, clay, or plaster. You can send out a design and have it cast. It's just that the vocabulary of today's furniture doesn't include that option, which is too bad. The cost is quite prohibitive, too. To cast four legs like this would be quite expensive.

PHS: This was a very expensive piece. It was being made for the 1925 Exposition so although there wasn't a king to pay for it as in the past, this was still made to represent the best that France could produce. International expositions took the place of royal commissions.

WC: These objects were going to be scrutinized by thousands of people, so they weren't going to cut corners in the quality of either the workmanship or materials.

PHS: This chair was shown with the desk in the 1925 Exposition.

WC: Where does the chair's form come from?

PHS: Again, you're getting a streamlined historical model, this time of a Louis XVI chair. This continuous arc from the hand rail to the seat rail is a nice invention. I like the way the feet, which look like blocks from the front, are actually stylized, cubed volutes.

WC: The scale is smaller than a Louis XVI chair, isn't it? It seems like such a tiny chair.

PHS: No, it's the same scale. Louis XVI chairs were smaller than the ample seats of the Louis XV period. Just as wood carvings were scaled down in the later period, so the same thing happened in furniture.

WC: It's solid ebony, not veneered. They certainly were pulling out all the stops with these two pieces.

Above, sketch by Emile-Jacques Ruhlmann

French Chair
Art Déco, c. 1925
Emile-Jacques Ruhlmann
(1879-1933)
Macassar ebony
H. 33-1/2, W. 17-1/2, D. 20
Metropolitan Museum of Art
Purchase, Edward C. Moore
Jr. Gift, 1926

RUHLMANN FURNITURE

PHS: Here we have three works by Emile-Jacques Ruhlmann, the quintessential Art Déco designer. The chair was a model that Ruhlmann used in his *Hôtel du Collectionneur* pavilion at the 1925 Paris Exposition. It's one of his best models. On the whole he was much less successful with chairs than with case pieces. He even did a three-legged one that fell over every time anyone sat in it.

WC: Is that the original upholstery?

PHS: Yes, Ruhlmann designed it himself. He did total interiors—he was an *ensemblier* as well as an *ébéniste.* He would design the wallpaper, the carpet, the curtains.

WC: This chair is solid ebony. See how the grain continues down the corners, how it curves? It would be close to impossible to do that with veneer.

PHS: Which makes it all the more a luxury item, because Macassar ebony was such an exotic wood.

WC: He got himself into a slight structural difficulty, though, trying to have such a thin apron. But I think it's really an elegant chair. It flows very nicely. Would this have been a dining room chair?

PHS: Ruhlmann featured them in the Grand Salon of the *Hôtel du Collectionneur,* which was a grandiose living room. But that doesn't mean he wouldn't have used the same model in a dining room.

WC: It's a graceful and refined chair, and it's not as based on tradition as the Süe and Mare chair.

PHS: It has quite a novel shoe, or *sabot.*

WC: Yes, I see it's fastened in with a screw in the center—pinned in on the side. It looks like it's slipped on.

PHS: And he used silvered bronze rather than gilt-bronze, which was a novelty. The floral marquetry cabinet is a major piece and Ruhlmann considered it as such. It was a knockout showpiece—it still is. The first design for it, dating to 1916, was shown in various salons; he kept exhibiting the same piece. He'd put it up on a little platform covered with fabric and set it off as an *objet d'art:* Art furniture with a capital A.

WC: Do you think he was personally responsible for the cabinet?

PHS: He designed it and supervised the construction. He was drawing all the time. He had a notebook and was constantly scribbling.

WC: I had a chance to see some of the drawings and I thought they were quite good. I had read that he wasn't much of a draftsman. They're doodles, but they're really good doodles. They're very understandable drawings.

PHS: He had draftsmen who developed his sketches into working drawings. Some years ago I visited one of the *chefs d'atelier* who were actually doing the woodworking for him and he said that Ruhlmann was really on top of his pieces, was always coming into the workshops—he had two of them—and looking at every piece of wood that was being worked on, throwing things out, starting things over again. So he was a constant presence in the making of his pieces. He originated the ideas, but then he also supervised every detail. He might not have been using his hand, but he was using his eye all the time.

WC: What's the function of this piece? Are there shelves inside?

PHS: Yes, there are three adjustable shelves, however the cabinet doesn't function very well if it's not full. The door is so heavy that when you open it the piece falls over. It's essentially a pictorial work of art, not a storage unit. I know, because when I discovered this furniture—literally, because I was an eighteenth century specialist assigned to work on twentieth century things and thought it was the end of the world!—I went down to the storeroom, got hold of the key to this, and then got caught. I opened the cabinet and it fell on top of me. I was converted to the beauty of Art Déco, but I learned its dangers as well!

WC: So this kind of piece was never used by anybody and no one ever complained about its not being useful.

PHS: Precisely. This piece was actually commissioned by the Metropolitan. I think the first version *was* more useful, because it was a triangular corner cabinet.

WC: Then it had more weight in the back, so it was less prone to fall over. But if it were going to be a showpiece, it's much better to do it this way, with four legs. This fits in front of any wall—you don't need a corner. The legs are so nicely done on these pieces.

PHS: Yes, to think they have concave facets—it's incredible. You're not even aware of all the concave and convex surfaces, because they look so simple and planar. There isn't ever a plane on Ruhlmann pieces, until you get into his works of the late '20s and early '30s.

WC: The floral design is handled as a marquetry pattern, not as inlay. The dots are, too. They didn't drill out holes in the wood

French Cabinet
Art Déco, 1926
Emile-Jacques Ruhlmann
(1879-1933)
Macassar ebony; marquetry
of ivory and amaranth wood
H. 50-1/4, W. 33-1/4, D. 14
Metropolitan Museum of Art
Purchase, Edward C. Moore
Jr. Gift, 1926

French Bedside Table
Art Déco, 1920-1930
Emile-Jacques Ruhlmann
(1879-1933)
Macassar ebony, ivory
H. 26, W. 19, D. 15
Metropolitan Museum of Art
Purchase, Rogers Fund, 1970

and hammer the ivory in later; they were placed in as the whole panel was being veneered.

PHS: Isn't it surprising that this marquetry held together, considering the bowed surface? After all, you have the ivory moving at a different rate of expansion than the wood.

WC: None of the ivory pieces is all that large—each is fairly small, so the curve over that distance is pretty minor. It's surprising to me that the ivory stayed in that long, because it's difficult to get ivory to adhere to a wood surface, even nowadays with epoxy.

PHS: Would they have used sandbags or steamed the ivory onto the surface?

WC: They wouldn't have had to steam it, but they might have put it on with hot sandbags or maybe they used a press that shape.

PHS: I think the contrast of the woods is very subtle—the amaranth in the marquetry and the ebony background.

WC: I personally couldn't build a piece that had that much of an emphasis on the pictorial image and was also useless.

PHS: It was purely an exhibition piece to show the technical mastery that Ruhlmann could achieve.

WC: I'm very sympathetic to the ornament—the ivory scrolls, the dots, the piano keyboard design on the top. It's only the flower that I object to, though I know the stylized floral form was one of the keynotes of Art Déco.

PHS: Ruhlmann wanted to be the master of a new style and this piece was asserting that mastery, saying "This is what Art Déco is all about." Its streamlined imagery and form, exquisite craftsmanship, and precious materials are the very definition of Art Déco in 1925, when the style was at its peak. People came away from the 1925 Exposition terming Ruhlmann the master. That's what he was after and that's what he got. On the other hand, there's more form and less picture to this bedside table of his.

WC: It *is* three-dimensional, whereas the cabinet is strictly frontal. And it does serve a useful purpose in an appropriate way.

PHS: Is it veneered on the inside?

WC: No, these are solid wood shelves, and they're adjustable. It almost seems like there should be a door on the front of it.

PHS: I don't think there ever was, because that's not the traditional form of a bedside table. It's lost its function completely because originally the open compartment of a night table was meant to contain a chamber pot.

WC: It's very difficult to make a piece like this—to put veneer all the way around a curved surface. But he didn't try to fit one piece all the way around. It is done very subtly in vertical strips. I imagine the leg is solid, but veneered over the front in order to get the grain pattern to continue.

PHS: The radial veneer on the top is masterful. It makes a beautiful sunburst pattern. The denticulation of ivory alternating with the dark wood veneer has a wonderful rhythm to it. Ruhlmann's best pieces are subtle but not boring.

WC: It's a fine little piece and, unlike the large cabinet, it's finished on all sides. It's got a back that you can look at.

PHS: The shaping of the legs is very pleasing. They flare out just a little and have a kind of animate stance. They don't just look like sticks.

WC: Were there originally two of these, one on each side of the bed?

PHS: I don't really know. Many of Ruhlmann's beds had night tables, but they were built into the headboard. The only reason we know this is a night table is because it has the traditional form of one.

WC: Was Ruhlmann's shop very modern? He could have had very sophisticated machinery and advanced tools—like presses.

PHS: I don't really know, but since his whole emphasis was on tradition and he wanted to equal the eighteenth century masters, perhaps he didn't take advantage of power tools. He certainly wouldn't want to publicize it if he did.

WC: Ruhlmann used oak for core wood very often, just like they did in the seventeenth and eighteenth centuries, and I was wondering why. In the 1700s they probably couldn't get any mahogany—which is a much better wood to work with—but by Ruhlmann's time they had access to the best mahogany, like Cuban mahogany, which is of very high quality and doesn't warp.

PHS: Mahogany was considered a luxury wood in France and the tradition throughout the centuries was to keep using it as such, even in the twentieth century when it was readily available.

WC: It's the same with the veneering process. I'm surprised Ruhlmann didn't use plywood or some other available material as a base.

PHS: It was a part of the mentality of the creation of the pieces: This is the way they did it in the golden past and that's the way we'll continue to do it.

WC: Ruhlmann's shop was becoming very aware of the problems of putting veneer directly over base material, though, so crossbanding was introduced, and sometimes even cross-banding twice, using a glue in between that allowed some movement between the layers.

PHS: What does crossbanding consist of?

WC: You would put down the first layer of veneer onto the base going in a different direction than the base. For instance, if the grain on the core wood went up and down, the first layer of veneer would go across, in the opposite direction. Then you'd put on another layer going in the opposite direction, and maybe even another. In a way, it's building a form of plywood. So I guess Ruhlmann did realize that tradition presented certain problems.

BRUNO PAUL DRESSING TABLE

PHS: This dressing table is by Bruno Paul, an architect who started out as a caricaturist—quite an odd transition. What I think is marvelous about this piece—and the reason I wanted it for the Museum—is that it's so Germanic. The high bourgeois taste of the 1920s and '30s in Germany has been overlooked. All the attention has been given to the Bauhaus, which was just one isolated group and aesthetic in Germany. Bruno Paul represented the silent majority. He was getting commissions for grand country houses in which he was trying to incorporate and update the German traditions, primarily the German Baroque. He was trying to modernize that history, the same way Süe and Mare were attempting to update French history. And I think their accomplishments are probably about parallel, though to my mind Ruhlmann easily surpasses both. The date on this piece is 1924, so he and Ruhlmann were working at the same time.

WC: You can't talk about it the same way you can about the Ruhlmann pieces, although I think the level of design is fine. It's got ivory pulls, but it's not a decorative element carried further, like the way Ruhlmann would put ivory feet on a piece as well. Too bad, because it would have benefited from ivory feet.

PHS: The ivory is added on as ornament rather than integrated into the design.

WC: Particularly those big knobs. They're not to scale.

PHS: But that's very much the scale of all Bruno Paul's interiors and buildings, very massive and heavy.

WC: Is there a tradition for this kind of leg form? It's straight and vertical until about halfway down, when it begins to curve.

PHS: Not that I know of. It's so exaggerated. The heart shape of the mirrored top holds the whole piece together. The entire set of furniture was an essay on the Tootsie Roll form. There was a tall chest of drawers that rippled like this all the way down. It's almost comical; it has a kind of jaunty quality to it.

WC: It's a pretty good quality piece and has such an interesting form, in my opinion.

PHS: The veneer doesn't, to my mind, correspond to any of the logic of cabinetwork. There are no mounts to protect the horizontal veneer on the sharp edges of the slender legs. We had both these pieces repaired about three times in the few

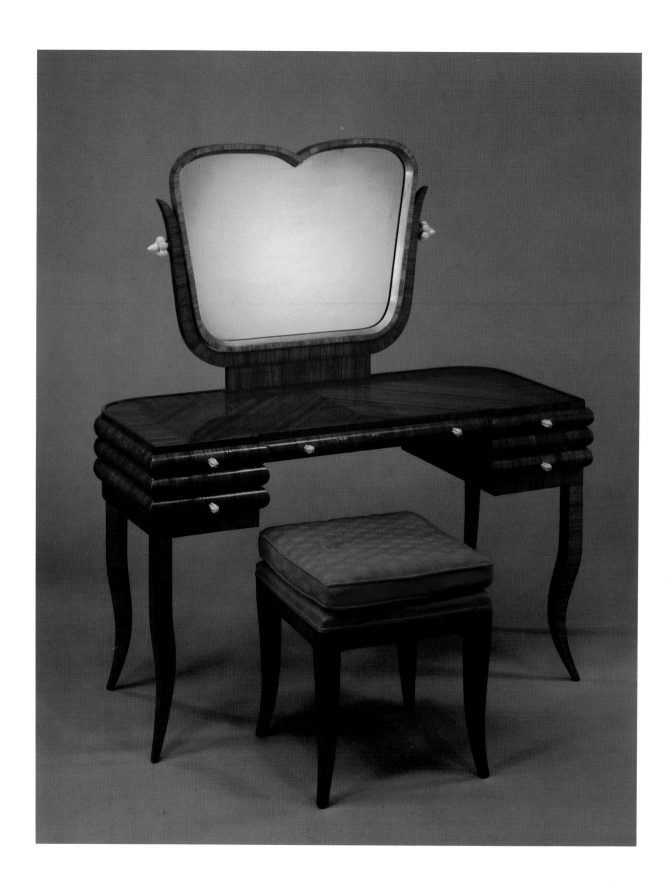

years we've had them. Just moving the stool in the storeroom it's lost some of the veneer on the legs. And all the bulging contours of the drawers have vertical veneer—how can you expect it to stay on those curves?

WC: It depends on how the veneer was prepared. If they steamed it, didn't just force it there, it would stay. I think it's susceptible to a problem, but it's not inevitable. It's not of the quality of the Ruhlmann pieces, but it is handmade and not a factory piece. These are hand-cut joints. But I agree with what you said about the feet—they look quite vulnerable. There's something perverse about running the grain in the wrong direction in both cases. You expect it to run horizontally on the top and vertically on the bottom, instead of the other way around.

PHS: Bruno Paul's work is very highly prized in Germany today. Almost all his buildings were destroyed in World War II, so every museum wants to have a piece of his furniture now. We're lucky to have this.

ROUSSEAU TABLE AND LEGRAIN STOOL

PHS: These two pieces, the Rousseau table and the Legrain stool, were designed for the studio of couturier Jacques Doucet. It was a total artistic environment completed in 1929 that included contemporary paintings and sculpture as well as African art. In 1912, Doucet sold his entire collection of superb eighteenth century French decorative arts and paintings at auction and began collecting avant-garde paintings—Picasso, Douanier Rousseau, and Braque—contemporary manuscripts and primitive African art. All his friends thought he was insane.

WC: So he wanted all new furniture to go with this new collection.

PHS: Right, he didn't want to live in the same kind of delicate, precious environment he had before. He wanted objects that were really sympathetic to the paintings and to the African art. So he got Pierre Legrain to be his chief interior decorator, and objects were commissioned from various artists, including Clément Rousseau, who designed this table.

WC: It's such a beautiful, elegant piece—and so modern.

PHS: The first version of it had been done for Robert de Rothschild; it's now in the Musée des Arts Décoratifs. Rousseau

German Dressing Table and Stool
Art Déco, c. 1924
Designed by Bruno Paul
(1874-1968); manufactured
by Herrmann Gerson, Berlin
Tulipwood, ivory, mirror glass
Table:
H. 53-1/2, W. 48-5/8, D. 21-1/4
Stool:
H. 20, W. 17-1/2, D. 17-1/2
Metropolitan Museum of Art
Gift of Ralph and Lester
Weindling, in memory of
Daly Weindling, 1976

got very little publicity in his day and, unfortunately, we know just a few of his pieces. But they're always very precious, jewel-like, and subtle. Of course, the use of precious materials—in this case ivory, ebony, and sharkskin—was characteristic of the Art Déco style. This is a seven-shark table, because Rousseau wanted the central segment of the skin—the belly, from which the imbrications radiate—to be an element repeated in the pattern. The table was practical as well, because sharkskin resists water, so you wouldn't have to worry too much about spilling a drink on its surface.

WC: I'd like to get a piece of sharkskin to work with sometime.

PHS: Ruhlmann used it, too, on a desk of his we have here at the Museum. It made a great writing surface.

WC: Is that why sharkskin is also known as shagreen, because it's green in color?

PHS: No, because it isn't actually green. This is just stained green. You also find it colored white or pink. It's naturally gray, I believe. There's an intriguing aside pertaining to this piece. When the restorer was working on it here a few years back, he noticed a slight irregularity of the grain underneath one corner. He found a religious medal of St. Thérèse-de-Lisieux, a Carmelite nun, neatly placed under that spot. After it was properly photographed and documented, it was put back in and covered up, so the artist's intent would not be violated.

WC: It's an interesting construction, the arms being used as handles and continuing down into the legs. The feet go inward ever so subtly. The ivory detail provides such a nice transition from the sharkskin to the ebony, too.

PHS: The signature and the date—1924—are scratched on it, but on the inside, covered by the metal braces under the corners. There may be more Clément Rousseau pieces around, but you have to take them apart to find out for sure. Poor Clément Rousseau, though, wasn't recognized for such a long time—just because they had the same first name and were working in the same period, he was confused with Clément Mère!

WC: Is this a traditional French form? Were there portable tables like this before?

PHS: There were small tables, but more like the Madame de Pompadour-style writing table that we looked at before. This serves a new and different function—it holds glasses of drinks, it's not for writing. You could move it and take it right to your chair—it's that light. With handles for legs it forms an ideogram of a portable table.

WC: It's very pleasing to look at from any angle.

PHS: And it represents something the French had been after since the Louis XV period—that seemingly improbable combination of delicacy and solidity. It's a very solid piece, even though it's on such skinny, hairpin legs.

WC: This stool obviously relates to African art.

PHS: It's inspired by an African chieftain's stool, but if you compare it to an actual primitive piece, you can see its stylization. It's the same kind of assimilation that you had in eighteenth century *chinoiserie* and then in nineteenth century *japonisme*. Legrain has turned the African form into a sophisticated geometric essay: the cubic blocks of the supports penetrated by six holes each, the triangles atop the cubes and again on the seat. The grain of the wood that's been hollowed out for the seat echoes the oval of the exterior contour.

WC: That's predictable. If you pick a straight-grained piece of wood and cut into it in a symmetrical way, you get those concentric, elliptical forms.

PHS: There's a total control and regularity of the gouged geometric motifs.

WC: It's very nicely done, very controlled.

French Stool
Art Déco, 1929
Pierre Legrain (1889-1929)
Rosewood
H. 12, W. 29, D. 9-3/4
Metropolitan Museum of Art
Purchase, Fletcher Fund, 1972

PHS: Which of these two pieces do you prefer as an aesthetic object?

WC: The table, because of its elegance and its refinement. Actually, it meets all my criteria for furniture. For one thing, it has a good consideration of function—it's a useful piece. Even the decoration on it is useful. There's sense behind the sharkskin, behind the ivory. Every part of the table has a rightness about it. The stool is a beautiful piece and I can appreciate it because it introduces the element of African art that's important to Art Déco, but the decoration on it is purely for decoration's sake, it doesn't have anything to do with making it useful.

PHS: I think the decoration is there because an African stool would have been decorated.

WC: But it's an African-looking, pseudo-African stool. I happen to think it's quite nice sculpturally, but I have to be pretty critical of it as a piece of furniture. It isn't going to sit too well, for one thing.

PHS: I think in a sense, like Bugatti's pieces, it exists first as an aesthetic object and then as a functional one. It will survive your using it, however—Bugatti's furniture won't. I think you're absolutely right about the Clément Rousseau piece. First, there's much more richness to it. You have a sort of introverted essay on a table and its function.

WC: It's perhaps the best piece in the whole show. It's absolutely the essence of everything that's important in furniture. Boiled down, nothing extra. But yet it responds so well to the basic human need for things to be decorated.

French Table
Art Déco, 1924
Clément Rousseau (1872-?)
Ebony, sharkskin, ivory
H. 29-1/2, W. 18-1/2, D. 18-1/2
Metropolitan Museum of Art
Purchase, Fletcher Fund, 1972

WENDELL CASTLE TWO SEATER

Editor's note: Below, Wendell Castle and Penelope Hunter-Stiebel talk about the final object from the Metropolitan's collection, Mr. Castle's *Two Seater,* and discuss some of their ideas on the furniture maker as artist.

PHS: As in the sculptor's process, you've built up the laminated cherrywood blocks of the *Two Seater,* then carved away and polished the form. The piece has a beautiful flow. It breaks with all chair making conventions, yet it has an almost organic

Overleaf:
American Two Seater
Studio Craft Movement, 1973
Wendell Castle (1932-   )
Cherrywood
H. 30-1/2, W. 60-1/2, D. 38
Metropolitan Museum of Art
Gift of Dr. and Mrs. Irwin
R. Berman, 1977

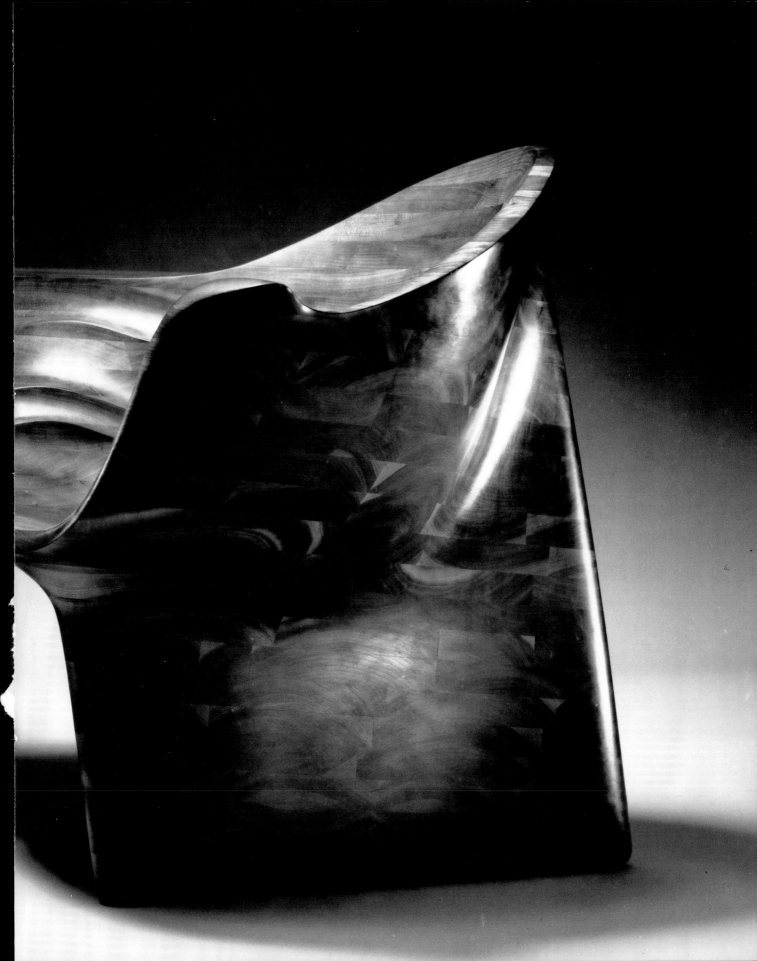

stability. What does the piece say to you, eight years later?
WC: I still see it as a form of extremism—something I feel I've always been involved with, ever since I began making furniture. Its extremism involves making a piece of furniture appear like sculpture.
PHS: What were the first types of things you did like?
WC: I worked with thin members abstractly, in a non-traditional, semi-functional way. I've been working with the same vocabulary for about eighteen years now. Very shortly after the thin, bent pieces came the thicker, heavier pieces. I did some fiberglass pieces in 1969-70, but I didn't think of that as an artistic direction. I was trying to get a base that could be produced and bring me some income—without my having to do it. Wood furniture I had to make myself; plastic, somebody else could do. But that didn't work. Today I'm doing things that are totally opposite: I'm going for the most expensive piece possible, made of the most exotic materials around and with the most superior workmanship possible. It's extreme—and I think extremism is where it's at.

The Clément Rousseau table we looked at was very exotic and very extreme. I'm not as interested in three-dimensional form right now—which is what the *Two Seater* is all about—but I'm still interested in giving a piece a personality, a presence. I think you can do that by giving it a proportion that's out of the ordinary. There are different high levels of craftsmanship and I think the level achieved in the *Two Seater* is different from the one achieved in my more recent pieces.

The levels of craftsmanship in the pieces we've been looking at are amazing. I used to be very uninterested in older furniture. I always concentrated on the twentieth century, thinking that's where all the activity was. I was most influenced previously by Art Nouveau furniture. It still excites me, but the more I learn about it, the more I feel there's an aspect to it that isn't one hundred percent right. There are some things missing—craftsmanship, for one. And a lot of the furniture is difficult to live with, because of its bizarre nature. The best examples—the ones that are the most interesting—are the ones that are the hardest to take.
PHS: But that's very true of Abstract Expressionist paintings, too. There are certain art forms where the message is not exactly positive. They shock, they're repulsive. Eighteenth century French furniture was the total opposite—it was a come-on, it didn't say "Stay away."

WC: It's not the form of the old furniture that interests me as much as the level of workmanship. I'm not surprised that anyone was able to think the forms up, but I *am* amazed that someone was actually able to execute them—and do it so well. Craftsmanship can be a form of extremism, even in the most traditional pieces. I've become quite taken with skill—in paintings as well as furniture. A whole reversal is happening, and not just in *my* mind. Beauty has become something you don't have to be ashamed of. It's happened in painting—people appreciating Alma-Tadema's work, for instance. When I was in college, if people said something was beautiful, that was the worst thing you could possibly say. I don't think that's a criticism anymore. It's just a big rearranging of values, of ideals—which always seems to occur in art. If I was going to paint something, I'd paint it the way it's supposed to be. I see more in Alma-Tadema than I do in Barnett Newman. I find I'm basically old-fashioned, I like the old things.

PHS: But isn't innovation a very important part in judging the level of achievement of a work of art? A lot of pieces we've been looking at that exhibit bravura, traditional craftsmanship were not made by the innovators of form—they were derived from prints or from the makers' having seen other pieces and elaborated on perhaps their technical aspects.

WC: They may not be innovative, but I'm amazed by the quality of workmanship in many of the older pieces. There's nothing made today that can amaze me in the slightest. There isn't anybody working today in furniture who does anything that I could consider amazing, in terms of level of workmanship. I'm inventing the form, but not *totally* inventing it. I'm working within the boundaries that are recognizable as furniture. Essentially, people who are working in ''art furniture'' today are in a mixed-up position. There's always a function somewhat sacrificed for art—the only basis left to judge it on is sculptural.

PHS: I think you can judge on the grounds of sensual appeal as well, which involves tactile as well as visual qualities. It doesn't depend on a supreme skill of, say, veneering or inlay, though you have to begin with a certain level of craftsmanship. It depends on being able to manipulate materials, to make something pleasing to the hand as well as to the eye. That's what Studio Craft Movement pieces like the *Two Seater* are about. I think there are still pinnacles to be reached in contemporary furniture making.

GLOSSARY

Abstract Expressionism — style of modern art in which the artist tries to convey emotions and ideas in a non-representational way.

Aesthetic Movement — informal art movement in England that thrived from the 1860s through the 1880s, wherein design was raised to the level of the so-called fine arts of painting, sculpture, and architecture. Japanese art and French painting influenced many of its artists. The movement spread to America in the 1880s.

Alma-Tadema, Sir Lawrence (1836-1912) — Dutch-born Victorian painter and designer who worked in England. His paintings of neoclassical subjects made him one of the most popular artists of his day.

amaranth — a South American wood, purplish in color, used for furniture.

architectonic — relating to the principles of architecture; resembling architecture in structure or organization.

Art Déco — name given in the 1960s to the decorative style of the 1920s, primarily in France, that was characterized by geometric shapes, stylized ornament, superior craftsmanship and materials, and—in its greatest works—a return to the ideals of French eighteenth century applied arts.

Art Nouveau — anti-historicizing architectural and decorative style that flourished in Europe at the turn of the century; characterized by curvilinear organic forms, seen to their best advantage in the works of Hector Guimard and the Ecole de Nancy.

l'Art Nouveau — Paris retail shop owned by entrepreneur Samuel Bing that gave the turn-of-the-century style its name. Among the artists whose works were sold by Bing were Edward Colonna and Louis Comfort Tiffany.

Arts and Crafts Movement — artistic movement with its origins in late nineteenth century England, specifically the ideas of William Morris, who urged craftsmen to return to medieval standards and techniques in opposition to the Industrial Age. Many American designers adopted these principles, among them the Tobey Furniture Company of Chicago and Gustave Stickley.

atelier — an artist's or designer's workshop or studio.

Baroque — seventeenth century design style characterized by exuberant decoration and curving forms; began in Italy, developed in a more classicizing vein under Louis XIV in France.

Bauhaus — German school of architecture, design, and decorative arts founded in 1919 at Weimar. Headed by architect Walter Gropius, this influential institution (literally, "build house") helped set the pace for the Modern Age. It was closed by Hitler in 1933.

Beaux-Arts — literally, "beautiful arts," the term describes objects rife with ornamentation derived from a variety of sources, mainly classical; especially prevalent in the Victorian period.

Bérain, Jean (1638-1711) — Belgian draftsman and designer whose decorative patterns resembling lacework were widely circulated throughout Europe and imitated on a variety of objects, including furniture and wall decorations; was named official designer to the king *(dessinateur du Roi)* by Louis XIV.

bergère — a winged armchair with upholstered sides, popular in France in the mid- and late eighteenth century.

Biennais, Martin-Guillaume (1764-1843) — French silversmith whose ateliers produced the most outstanding silver and gilt-bronze works of the Empire period, as well as some woodwork and furniture.

Bing, Samuel (1838-1905) — German entrepreneur whose Paris gallery, *l'Art Nouveau,* gave its name to a new style of art—as well as introducing the works of Gallé, Colonna, and Tiffany to an eager public.

bois de bout — end grain of wood, cut from small branches.

bombé — French term for furniture with convex shapes, notably the front of a commode; also applied to any curved or swelling shape.

Boucher, Francois (1703-1770) — French Rococo painter who was a favorite of Madame de Pompadour. Besides producing a number of portraits of his patron, Boucher made tapestry designs and painted mythological scenes.

Boulle, André-Charles (1642-1732) — the first great French *ébéniste,* who worked in the Louis XIV period; known for his elaborate pieces with tortoiseshell and brass marquetry (works of this type have come to be known as Boulle work).

Braque, Georges (1882-1963) — French painter often credited, along with Picasso, with the development of Cubism.

Bugatti, Carlo (1855-1940) — Italian furniture designer whose imaginative, exotic pieces were heavily ornamented, mostly with Eastern- and Near Eastern-type decoration.

bureau plat — a large, flat-topped writing table.

burning — design on wood done with a heated tool, similar to branding.

burnish — to make something shiny or glossy, especially by polishing or rubbing.

cabinetmaker — a skilled woodworker who makes fine furniture.

calligraphic — resembling beautiful, elegant handwriting.

cantilevered — supported at one end by a projecting beam or member, as in a chair.

carcass — the under-structure of a piece of furniture, i.e., that over which a layer of veneer is applied.

cartouche — ornate frame motif that became the hallmark of the Rococo style.

casket — a small box or chest, as for jewelry or letters.

chaise courante — in eighteenth century France, a lightweight chair intended to be moved about in a room to allow for social grouping.

chaise meublante — in eighteenth century France, a heavy chair meant to remain against a wall as part of the formal decoration of a room.

Charles II (1630-1685) — King of England from 1660-1685.

chasing — ornamental engraving on metal, especially associated with gilded mounts.

chef d'atelier — chief craftsman or foreman in charge of an atelier, or workshop.

Ch'ing Dynasty — a Manchu dynasty in China dating from 1644-1912; the last imperial dynasty.

chinoiserie — style in Western art inspired by Oriental art.

Chippendale, Thomas (1718-1779) — one of the best-known English furniture makers and author of the first comprehensive book of furniture designs.

chisel — a metal tool with a cutting edge, used with a hammer in shaping stone, metal, or wood.

classical — of or relating to the culture of the ancient Greek or Roman world; traditional.

Collet, Edouard-Louis (1876-?) — Swiss-born wood carver who worked in France in the Art Nouveau period.

Colonna, Edward (1862-1948) — German-born Art Nouveau designer who worked in Belgium and America before being employed by Samuel Bing in Paris as a furniture and jewelry designer; returned to America in 1905.

commode — a chest of drawers on legs, a furniture form developed in France in the early eighteenth century.

console table — a table fixed to a wall and only partly supported by its legs.

core wood — wood onto which veneer is glued; carcass.

crest rail — horizontal top rail on the back of a chair.

Cromwell, Oliver (1599-1658) — English statesman. He overthrew Charles I to install the Commonwealth and was Lord Protector of England from 1653 to 1658.

crossbanding — technique of applying layers of veneer to the core wood, the grain of each going in the opposite direction from the one below; can comprise two or more layers.

crowned C — mark stamped on gilt-bronze in France between 1745 and 1749 signifying payment of a tax.

Crystal Palace — giant glass-and-iron construction in London erected as the showplace for the Great Exhibition of 1851.

Cubism — style of abstract art that fragmented objects into their geometric components. Cubist painters attempted to depict several views of one subject on a two-dimensional plane.

dado — the lower part of a wall that is often paneled and set off by moldings.

de Forest, Lockwood (1850-1932) — American artist and designer who was a partner in Louis C. Tiffany & Associated Artists; in 1881, founded workshops in India to produce ornaments and exotic carved, inlaid furniture for his New York decorating studio.

Delacroix, Eugène (1798-1863) — French painter who rejected classicism and became a leader of the Romantic style; often depicted exotic subjects.

Delftware — tin-glazed Dutch earthenware with blue-and-white or polychrome decoration; by extension, English earthenware in the same style.

demilune — half moon.

Denon, Dominique Vivant (1747-1825) — French diplomat, collector, and engraver who was an influential figure in the court of Napoleon; director of the Musée Napoléon.

denticulation — a series of small rectangular blocks that project like teeth.

Doucet, Jacques (1853-1929) — Paris couturier and avid art collector.

dowel — peg on a piece of wood meant to fit into a corresponding hole on another piece of wood.

draftsman — one who draws plans and sketches, as for furniture or buildings.

Dubois, Jacques (1693-1763) — Paris *ébéniste* working in the Rococo style.

ébéniste — furniture maker who excells in the art of veneering; usually referring to eighteenth and nineteenth century French craftsmen, but also applied to later artists, such as Emile-Jacques Ruhlmann.

ébénisterie — the art of making veneered furniture.

Ecole de Nancy — school of Art Nouveau that developed at Nancy, in the French province of Lorraine, under the leadership of Emile Gallé. Gallé exhorted his colleagues—including Louis Majorelle—to derive their ornament from the direct study of nature.

en suite — in a succession, set, or series.

end grain — wood cut across the grain, as distinguished from wood cut along the grain.

engraving — decorating by incision, as on metal or wood.

ensemblier — decorator responsible for creating the total design of an interior, i.e., curtains, walls, furniture, etc.

l'Exposition Internationale des Arts Décoratifs et Industriels Modernes — 1925 World's Fair held in Paris that marked the apogee of the style that was dubbed in the 1960s Art Déco, and whence the style received its name. Among the artists whose pavilions received acclaim were Emile-Jacques Ruhlmann and Süe and Mare.

facet — anything resembling the small, polished surface of a gem.

fillet — a narrow band or strip of a material.

fleur-de-lis — French term for a stylized lily flower; at one time the royal arms of France.

fondeur-ciseleur — metal worker who cast and finished the surface of bronzes for interior decoration. The profession reached its peak in eighteenth century France.

French polishing — term used for a type of polishing that entails hand-rubbing the surface of furniture with numerous layers of polish.

fret — an ornamental network comprising small straight bars intersecting one another in right angles.

fretsaw — a narrow-bladed, fine-toothed saw held under tension in a frame and used for cutting curved outlines.

Gallé, Emile (1846-1904) — French glass artist and furniture designer who was a leader of the Art Nouveau style, specifically its Ecole de Nancy group.

gallery — a railing or raised lip along the edge of a table.

Gérôme, Jean-Léon (1824-1904) — French artist best known for his depictions of classical subjects; also painted Oriental genre scenes.

gesso — a paste prepared by mixing pulverized chalk or limestone with size or glue and spread upon a surface to ready it for painting or gilding.

Gibbons, Grinling (1648-1721) — English Baroque sculptor best known for his wood carvings.

gild — to decorate with thinly applied gold.

Godwin, Edward (1833-1886) — English designer and architect known for his Anglo-Japanese furniture.

gold leaf — a thin sheet of gold applied to surfaces, such as on wood panels.

goldsmith — one who makes articles out of gold, especially jewelry.

grain — the stratification of fibers in a piece of wood.

grille — a grating that forms a screen or barrier and is often ornamental.

guild — trade association of craftsmen or merchants; begun in medieval times and intended to keep standards high and look out for the best interests of its members.

Guimard, Hector (1867-1942) — French Art Nouveau architect and designer whose flamboyant style made him one of the movement's most distinctive exponents; among his projects were the entranceways to the Paris Métro.

Hepplewhite, George (d. 1786) — English Neoclassical furniture maker who achieved posthumous fame with the publication of his book of furniture designs.

Herter Brothers — New York furniture making establishment founded c. 1865 by German-born Gustave Herter and his brother Christian (1840-1883); made Japanese-style furniture as well as elaborate art furniture commissioned by America's rich.

l'Hôtel du Collectionneur — pavilion designed by Emile-Jacques Ruhlmann at the 1925 Paris Exposition. One of the fair's most popular attractions, it exhibited the work of some of the top artists of the Art Déco period—all set in the imaginary dwelling of a wealthy connoisseur.

huang hua-li — Southeast Asian rosewood found in Chinese furniture.

hygroscopic — absorbing or attracting moisture from the air.

ideogram — a picture or symbol representing a thing or idea but not a particular word or phrase for it.

imbrication — an overlapping of edges, as in fish scales or roof tiles.

inlay — to form a decorative pattern by setting small pieces of a foreign material into recesses carved out of a surface; on furniture, the material can be wood, ivory, mother-of-pearl, etc. Also, a decorative pattern formed in such a way.

intertwined L's — French royal monogram comprising one L overlapping its reversed image; adopted by Louis XIV and used by Louis XV and XVI.

Jacob, Georges (1739-1814) — French furniture maker, one of the leading *menuisiers* during the reign of Louis XVI.

Jacob-Desmalter, François-Honoré-Georges (1770-1841) — French furniture maker, son of Georges Jacob and one of the best-known craftsmen of the Empire.

japonisme — the adaptation of Japanese designs in the West, especially in the late nineteenth century.

Jensen, Gerreit (worked c. 1680-1715) — Dutch-born cabinetmaker who worked at the English court and greatly influenced furniture making in the William and Mary period.

jog — a projecting part.

joiner — a person who constructs articles by joining pieces of wood.

joint — the junction of two or more members of a formed structure, as in a chair.

laminate — to put together superposed layers of wood, bonding them with an adhesive and compressing them under heat.

lap joint — a joint made by overlapping two ends or edges and fastening them together.

Legrain, Pierre (1889-1929) — French Art Déco decorator primarily known for his bookbindings; also designed furniture influenced by African and Cubist art.

Leighton, Lord Frederick (1830-1896) — English Victorian painter whose monumental compositions often depicted mythological subjects.

Lévy-Dhurmer, Lucien (1865-1953) — Algerian-born French artist, primarily known for his Symbolist paintings and pastels; also designed ceramics and interiors.

Louis XIV (1638-1715) — King of France who reigned from 1643 to 1715 and established the French nation-state and the monarchy as a political system; associated with the French Baroque style.

Louis XV (1710-1774) — King of France who reigned from 1715 to 1774; associated with the French Rococo style.

Louis XVI (1754-1793) — King of France who reigned from 1774 to 1792; associated with the French Neoclassical style.

Madame de Pompadour (1721-1764) — official mistress of Louis XV and important tastemaker in the French Rococo period.

maître — craftsman achieving the rank of master in a guild.

Majorelle, Louis (1859-1926) — French cabinetmaker who designed Art Nouveau furniture; a member of the Ecole de Nancy.

Mare, André (1885-1932) — French Art Déco designer, co-founder of the Compagnie des Arts Français, along with Louis Süe. Originally trained as a painter, he returned to painting after the Compagnie closed down in 1928.

Marquand, Henry (1819-1902) — second president of the Metropolitan Museum of Art and a patron of the arts in the late nineteenth century.

marquetry — technique in which elaborate patterns are formed like a jigsaw puzzle by the insertion of pieces of material—wood, shell, ivory, and the like—into a wood veneer that is then applied to another surface.

Mary (1662-1694) — Queen of England who reigned with her husband William III from 1689 until her death.

mask — head or face used as an ornament, often grotesque.

master — a craftsman achieving the highest rank in a guild system, usually after serving terms as apprentice and journeyman; in French, *maître*.

Meissonnier, Juste-Aurèle (c. 1693-1750) — French Rococo designer who worked as an architect and silversmith but is best known for his engraved designs, which were circulated throughout Europe.

menuiserie — the art of making furniture of solid wood.

menuisier — furniture maker specializing in carved furniture, as opposed to an *ébéniste,* whose specialty is veneered pieces.

Mère, Clément (1870-?) — French Art Déco furniture maker whose works were elaborately inlaid and very often utilized decorative panels of tooled leather.

Ming Dynasty — a Chinese dynasty dating 1368-1643 and marked in the arts by the perfection of established techniques.

molding — a curved strip or plane used for ornamentation or finishing.

monolithic — resembling a single monumental stone.

Moorish — inspired by Islamic art; a decorating style popular in the late nineteenth century in Britain and America characterized by fringes, tassels, brocades, and the like.

mount — a metal attachment on a piece of furniture, often both functional and decorative, such as a drawer pull, keyhole plate, or sheath on a table leg.

Neoclassical — style employing the Greek repertory of ornament that succeeded the Rococo style in the late eighteenth century; characterized by restrained rectilinear forms.

Newman, Barnett (1905-1970) — American abstract painter best known for huge canvases of color fields inflected with bands of other colors.

nouvelle vague — new wave.

objet d'art — a functional or purely decorative three-dimensional article prized for its beauty.

ormolu — covered with a thin layer of gold; used in the eighteenth century for furniture mounts or articles of interior decoration, such as andirons and wall-lights.

ornemaniste — court-appointed designer of decorations in France.

oyster veneer — type of veneer of Dutch origin that resembles oyster shells placed side by side; effect achieved by laying down strips of wood cut from small branches.

palisander — type of wood that is hard, dark, and purplish; similar to rosewood.

palmette — ornament of Greek derivation based on the branch of a date palm.

Parent, Aubert (1753-1835) — French architect and sculptor who specialized in still-life reliefs in wood.

pattern book — album of engravings published and circulated to serve as design models, thus familiarizing craftsmen with new styles.

Paul, Bruno (1874-1968) —German architect, caricaturist, and designer whose work evolved from Art Nouveau at the turn of the century to Art Déco in the 1920s.

paw foot — terminal on the leg of a piece of furniture in the shape of an animal—usually a lion's—foot.

Percier, Charles (1764-1838) — French designer who, along with his collaborator Pierre-François-Léonard Fontaine, was responsible for the development of the French Empire style.

plinth — architectural term for the projecting base of a wall or column.

plywood — a structural material comprising crossbanded sheets of wood.

polychromed — decorated in several colors.

Poynter, Sir Edward John (1836-1919) — English painter; director of the National Gallery in London from 1881 to 1894.

prototype — an original model on which something is patterned, an archetype; a first full-scale and usually functional form of a new type or design of a construction.

purfling — ornamentation, such as inlay or openwork, on the border or edges of an object; e.g., the decoration around the holes of a stringed instrument.

pylon — a rectangular pyramidal tower, such as those flanking temple gateways in ancient Egyptian architecture.

quillwork — pen engraving, as on a piece of furniture.

racking — being forced out of shape or out of plumb.

Régence — transitional French decorative style coming between Baroque and Rococo, c. 1715-1725; roughly corresponds to the minority of Louis XV, who ascended the throne at the age of five.

relief — projecting ornament, as in bas-relief (low relief).

repareur — artisan whose job was to apply gesso to wood as the basis for gilding.

repoussé — ornamental metalwork hammered out into relief form from the back.

Richardson, Henry Hobson (1838-1886) — American architect who worked in a neo-Romanesque style. The Marshall Field Building in Chicago was one of his greatest projects.

Rococo — style of decoration in the eighteenth century identified in France with Louis XV; characterized by extravagant scroll work and asymmetry, informality and light-hearted gaiety.

rose metal — alloy made of bismuth, lead, and tin with a very low melting point of 95 ° C.

roundel — a small decorative disc or medallion.

Rousseau, Clément (1872-?) — French Art Déco furniture designer known for his use of luxurious materials.

Rousseau, Henri, called "Douanier" (1844-1910) — painter whose strong naive vision caught the fancy of modern art lovers.

Ruhlmann, Emile-Jacques (1879-1933) — French *ébéniste-ensemblier* whose furniture represents the highest form of the Art Déco style.

sabot — literally, "clog," a term used to refer to the caps on furniture feet, usually bronze but sometimes, as in Ruhlmann pieces, ivory.

Salon — annual exhibition of works of art.

sandbox — a receptacle with shaker containing loose sand to be sprinkled on wet ink; standard item of equipment for eighteenth century letter writing.

scribe — to mark a line on by cutting or scratching with a pointed instrument.

scroll — a spiral termination.

seaweed marquetry — type of marquetry in the form of sprays of sea plants; found on English and Dutch furniture in the late 1600s and early 1700s.

shagreen — the rough skin of sharks and rays, often dyed green or other colors and used as decoration on furniture and accessories.

Sheraton, Thomas (1751-1806) — English cabinetmaker who owes his fame to his books of furniture designs.

splat — a central vertical member of the back of a chair.

stencil — to produce a design on a surface by applying a pigment through a perforated or cut-out sheet of paper or metal.

stipple — to engrave by means of flicks and dots; to apply by repeated touches.

streamline — to design or construct with a smooth, flowing line; to modernize, bring up-to-date.

stretcher — a crossbar or rung connecting two legs, as on a chair or table.

strip — to remove the outer surface of a decorative panel or piece of furniture, usually paint and gesso, thus exposing the wood underneath.

strut — a crosspiece designed for structural support.

Studio Craft Movement — current movement in America, begun after World War II, whose artists choose traditional techniques of crafting wood, ceramics, glass, metal, and fiber as their means of artistic expression.

stylized — conforming to a conventional style; represented or designed according to a style or stylistic pattern rather than according to nature.

Süe, Louis (1875-1968) — French Art Déco furniture designer and decorator who was trained as an architect; co-founder of the Compagnie des Arts Français.

Sullivan, Louis (1856-1924) — American architect working out of Chicago whose interior decoration was characterized by feathery vegetable forms.

sunburst — decoration in which rays radiate out from the center.

Symbolism — late nineteenth century movement that embraced literature, music, and art, and concerned itself with the true meaning of life and nature through internalized processes of suggestions and symbols.

tambour — a rolling front or top of a piece of furniture comprising narrow strips of wood glued on canvas.

Tiffany, Louis Comfort (1848-1933) — American Art Nouveau-period designer best known for his works in glass, but also responsible for interior, metal, pottery, and furniture designs. Established Louis C. Tiffany & Associated Artists in 1879; in 1890 the firm became Tiffany Glass & Decorating Company and in 1900 it was known simply as Tiffany Studios.

Tobey Furniture Company — large Chicago furniture manufacturing company founded in 1875 by brothers Charles and Frank Tobey.

Toro, Jean-Bernard, also known as **Turreau** (1672-1731) — French sculptor from the port city of Toulon who started out doing sculpture for ships and by extension turned to carving wood and making pieces of furniture. The use of carved masks was popularized through engravings of his furniture designs.

upright — a vertical element.

Van Risenburgh, Bernard, also known as **Vanrisamburgh** (c. 1700-1765) — French Rococo *ébéniste* whose designs are marked by elegance and refinement; produced pieces for Louis XV and Madame de Pompadour. Long identified only by his signature "BVRB."

Vanderbilt, William H. (1821-1885) — American financier, philanthropist, and patron of the arts.

varnish — a liquid preparation that when spread and allowed to dry on a surface forms a hard, lustrous, and usually transparent coating.

vellum — a fine-grained unsplit lambskin, kidskin, or calfskin.

veneer — a thin sheet of figured wood of superior grain attached to the surface of a usually inferior wood; to overlay a common wood with a thin layer of finer wood for outer finish or decoration.

Versailles — royal country mansion outside Paris expanded by Louis XIV into a great palace and seat of government.

Vivant-Denon, Dominique — See Denon, Dominique Vivant.

volute — a spiral or scroll-shaped form.

Watt, William (worked c. 1865-1885) — London furniture manufacturer best known for his execution of the Anglo-Japanese designs of Edward Godwin.

Wilde, Oscar (1854-1900) — English writer with a flamboyant style. He helped spread the tenets of the Aesthetic Movement in America on an 1880s lecture tour.

William of Orange (1650-1702) — Dutch-born ruler who, as William III, was co-regent with Mary II, Queen of England, from 1689 until her death in 1694; King of England from 1694-1702.